FILM STARS

Stars are an integral part of every major film industry in the world.
In this pivotal new series, each book is devoted to an international
movie star, looking at the development of their identity, their acting
and performance methods, the cultural significance of their work,
and their influence and legacy. Taking a wide range of different stars,
including George Clooney, Brigitte Bardot and Dirk Bogarde
among others, this series encompasses the sphere of silent and sound
acting, Hollywood and non-Hollywood areas of cinema, and child and
adult forms of stardom. With its broad range, but a focus throughout
on the national and historical dimensions to film, the series offers
students and researchers a new approach to studying film.

SERIES EDITORS
Martin Shingler and Susan Smith

PUBLISHED TITLES
Barbara Stanwyck *Andrew Klevan*
Brigitte Bardot *Ginette Vincendeau*
Carmen Miranda *Lisa Shaw*
Elizabeth Taylor *Susan Smith*
Hanna Schygulla *Ulrike Sieglohr*
Mickey Rourke *Keri Walsh*
Nicole Kidman *Pam Cook*
Penélope Cruz *Ann Davies*
Star Studies: A Critical Guide *Martin Shingler*

Rock HUDSON

JOHN MERCER

A BFI book published by Palgrave

First published in 2015 by
PALGRAVE

on behalf of the

BRITISH FILM INSTITUTE
21 Stephen Street, London W1T 1LN
www.bfi.org.uk

There's more to discover about film and television through the BFI. Our world-renowned archive, cinemas, festivals, films, publications and learning resources are here to inspire you.

PALGRAVE in the UK is an imprint of Macmillan Publishers Limited, registered in England, company number 785998, of 4 Crinan Street, London N1 9XW. Palgrave Macmillan in the US is a division of St Martin's Press LLC, 175 Fifth Avenue, New York, NY 10010. Palgrave is a global imprint of the above companies and is represented throughout the world. Palgrave® and Macmillan® are registered trademarks in the United States, the United Kingdom, Europe and other countries.

Designed by couch
Cover images: (front) *Seconds* (John Frankenheimer, 1966), © Paramount Pictures Corporation/ Joel Productions/Gibraltar Productions; (back) *All That Heaven Allows* (Douglas Sirk, 1955), © Universal Pictures Company

Set by Cambrian Typesetters, Camberley, Surrey
Printed in China

This book is printed on paper suitable for recycling and made from fully managed and sustained forest sources. Logging, pulping and manufacturing processes are expected to conform to the environmental regulations of the country of origin.

British Library Cataloguing-in-Publication Data
A catalogue record for this book is available from the British Library
A catalog record for this book is available from the Library of Congress

978-1-84457-464-3

(*previous page*) Rock Hudson and Jane Wyman
in *All That Heaven Allows*

CONTENTS

ACKNOWLEDGMENTS

I would like first and foremost to thank Martin Shingler for asking me to write this book in the first place and for reigniting an enthusiasm for an actor and a group of films that have played an important part in my life.

I must also extend my thanks and gratitude to my colleagues in the Birmingham School of Media and the Birmingham Centre for Media and Cultural Research. I have benefited not only emotionally by the enthusiasm and commitment of the team of scholars that I work alongside but also in practical terms as I was lucky enough to secure a sabbatical to support the research that is the basis of this publication.

I would like to additionally acknowledge my gratitude to the members of the Melodrama Research Group at the University of Kent who have generously invited me to speak about my research and allowed me to become an honorary member.

Thanks also to the staff of the BFI Library for helping me to locate archival materials and to the members of the online archive, the Rock Hudson Project, which has been a goldmine of ephemera, inspiration and leads.

Finally, thanks go to Trevor for everything else and more besides.

INTRODUCTION

Tall, dark and handsome, Rock Hudson represented the Hollywood ideal of American masculinity during the 1950s and 60s; an ideal that was to be questioned and ultimately undermined during the years to follow. Masculinity was always at the heart of Rock Hudson's star persona and his performances in cinema and television. It is probably true to say that Hudson, more than almost any other actor of his generation, was presented as the paradigmatic example of the 'all American' heterosexual male; handsome, athletic, impeccably groomed, solid and dependable, a strong deep voice and a performance style that embodies stoicism, he was all things that men were expected to aspire to and women (it was assumed) adored.

Inevitably then one of the motivating factors that lies behind writing this book is a working out of my own understanding of what Rock Hudson means as an actor and as an icon of his era. One of the first films I ever saw in a cinema was a 1972 matinee rerun of the Rock Hudson and Doris Day comedy of 1964 *Send Me No Flowers*. I can vividly remember the glamorous vision of suburban affluence that the film offered, Hudson and Day's luxuriously appointed home and the immaculately groomed appeal of the two stars. Day and Hudson seemed, to me at least, to exemplify exactly what a couple should be like: funny, attractive and, of course, rich. A visit to the cinema, especially to see releases from the 1950s and 60s, was however a relatively rare occurrence and, like many people whose childhood and adolescence spanned the 1970s and early 80s, many of my earliest experiences of Hollywood film were gained via television. While I was growing up it was common to see films from the 1930s, 40s and 50s broadcast back to back on Saturday and Sunday afternoons and in school holidays. This meant that my education in film history began here, in the home and on the TV screen. Paradoxically, that meant that the cinema of the past was in fact my *present* in terms of the material I was most often exposed to. The narrative constructions, dreams of glamour and most of all the gender roles of Classical Hollywood made a very profound and lasting impact on me and young people like me.

Additionally like many other gay men of my generation, becoming an adolescent in the 1970s meant that I experienced some degree of confusion and guilt about my own sexuality. This is, naturally enough, largely to do with the wider culture of the period and the experience of a childhood in a provincial British city where homosexuality was only ever discussed in the most disparaging and phobic of terms. Hollywood cinema, however, also had a part to play, as this was where so many of us derived our understanding of what it meant to be a 'real' man or woman. Rock Hudson as far as the general public was concerned was most definitely a 'real' man but the masculinity he represented was not quite as straightforward as it might seem. His masculinity was not the taciturn and surly model offered by John Wayne, for example. Neither was he the strident testosterone-driven exemplar epitomised by Kirk Douglas or Charlton Heston. There was instead a quiet, internalised 'gentle' masculinity to Hudson, a 'natural' quality (often explicitly connected to nature) that I can remember well and which seemed to offer a way to be a man that was not about aggression, fist fights and shoot-outs.

This 'natural' embodied masculinity was eventually to be complicated of course by the accounts of Hudson's private life and the suppressed 'revelations' about his homosexuality that emerged following his death from AIDS-related illness at the height of the first wave of the crisis in 1985. My mother, who grew up in the 1950s and 60s still claims that she cannot believe that Rock Hudson was gay. This is neither a denial of homosexuality nor an expression of homophobia. Rather it demonstrates the extent to which Hudson's star persona, enshrined in his performances in film and television over forty years, was intricately bound up with notions of what the 'ideal' heterosexual male looked, spoke and acted like. As Richard Dyer notes in an essay that discusses the reading of Hudson's star image, 'Neither in looks nor in performance style does Rock conform to 1950s and 1960s notions of what gay men are like' (2001: 162). Inevitably the circumstances that surrounded the end of Hudson's life had a destabilising effect on the reception of Hudson as a film star and this has perhaps meant that his contribution to film culture and his work as an actor has not received the critical attention afforded many of his contemporaries.

In this book, my aim is to reclaim Rock Hudson as an important film actor and identify the specific qualities of both his performances and his image that made him one of the most popular and successful male film stars of his generation. Hudson is not usually regarded in critical accounts as a great actor (even though he received an Oscar nomination in 1956 for *Giant*) and my intention here is not to make such a hyperbolic claim. He is nonetheless an important actor and an important figure in cinema history for several reasons but largely because his construction as a star, his performances and his career reveal a great deal about the nature of American popular culture and attitudes towards gender and sexuality during the years when his career started, his ascent to stardom in the 1950s and early 60s and his later career on TV during the 70s. With a name concocted by his agent, intended to connote images of solidity and permanence and his equally scrupulously designed professional image, Hudson seems like the supreme example of the manufactured Hollywood star from a period where the studio system was in rapid and terminal decline. It has become a commonplace to suggest that he is the epitome (alongside actors like the aforementioned John Wayne and Charlton Heston) of a moribund masculinity in the face of a more questioning model of manhood offered by James Dean, Marlon Brando and Paul Newman. My intention is to interrogate and question some of the assumptions that lie behind what was to become the orthodox account and by so doing to recuperate Hudson as a star who embodies the period of transition between the old Hollywood and the new. My aim here is to consider Hudson as an actor whose work and image reveal levels of representational and cultural complexity that are richer and more ambiguous than the standard account seems to suggest. As Hudson's long-time friend George Nader was to note, 'There *is* no Rock Hudson. There are *many* Rock Hudsons' (Davidson and Hudson 1986: 6).

This book is organised into three chapters that are largely determined by the various stages in Hudson's career. The first chapter focuses on the early career of the aspiring film actor, his training and relationships with his agent Henry Willson and the director Raoul Walsh. This chapter reveals a young actor experimenting with performance styles and a studio working to establish a career based around performances in a range of generic contexts. The second chapter begins with Hudson's transition from supporting player to fully fledged star as a result of his role in *Magnificent Obsession* in 1954. The chapter looks at the personnel involved in the construction of his star persona and the refinement of his performance style during this period. The third and final chapter has a broader scope and discusses the commodification of Hudson's image, his move into comic acting during the 1960s and roles that extended his dramatic repertoire during the mid-60s and early 70s. In this final chapter, the fortunes of the 'mature' actor are also discussed alongside Hudson's career transition into television in the

1970s. The perceived disparity between his public persona and what was later alleged to be his 'true' nature as a promiscuous homosexual male (and the first Hollywood star to die as a result of AIDS) is discussed in postscript. Here I explore how Hudson's signification was radically altered and how (and why) he was claimed as a text for analysis by queer theorists.

1 THE APPRENTICESHIP, 1948–54

Hudson's first screen performance was as an uncredited, supporting player in the role of an air corps officer in *Fighter Squadron* (1948). It has become part of his popular legend that, with only three lines of dialogue, the young actor had taken anything between twenty and thirty-eight takes (depending on which source you choose to believe) to successfully deliver his lines, much to the frustration of the famously brusque director Raoul Walsh. This frequently recounted incident has, in many respects, tended to set the tone in terms of the critical reception of Hudson's subsequent screen performances.

Chosen primarily for his physical appearance and disparagingly referred to as 'good scenery' by Walsh who, as we will see in this chapter, had a significant role in fashioning his star image and his emergent performance style, Hudson has frequently been caricatured as a weak actor (Moss 2011: 281). For example, in a documentary about the star, fellow contract player William Reynolds notes that, in the early years of his career, 'I don't think that many of us thought he was that much of an actor … I don't think my opinion of Rock was of an actor of any great moment. I thought he was awkward at times.'[1] This is an opinion, however, that Reynolds suggests he was to eventually revise. Similarly, Robert Stack, who appeared in *Fighter Squadron* with Hudson, remembers Walsh describing Hudson as a 'silly, black haired goon'. Jack Larson, the star of *Fighter Squadron*, remembers Hudson's stage fright and on-set nerves, which would evidently account for the untrained novice's performance. According to Larson, he 'would stumble, would gulp, would forget the lines, he wouldn't come in. It was an unbelievable situation.' This characterisation of Hudson's acting extends itself to film scholarship. In an essay on Hudson and Day's collaborations, Foster Hirsch describes Hudson in his early roles as demonstrating 'no discernible acting skill whatsoever' as 'the wooden new actor with the trick name' and perhaps most critically that 'Hudson still didn't seem to grasp what it took to create the semblance of a human being on film' (2010: 157). This kind of dismissive summary of Hudson's work and the wider concomitant debate around the nature and quality of Hollywood film acting is a subject that we will return to on more than one occasion in this book.

As I have indicated in the Introduction, at least one of the objectives of this book is to recuperate Hudson's reputation as an actor and, in so doing, to both reappraise and situate his performances within a context that might account for them. This chapter deals ostensibly with the material upon which many of the charges of bad acting are largely based and is an attempt to challenge (or at least question) the orthodox view of Hudson's acting prowess. This means focusing attention on a series of early performances in a range of genre films of variable quality and intent. My contention here is that this is the period where we are able to witness the developmental stages of a performance style, largely through a process of trial and error. This involved experimentation with different styles, registers and material as key personnel in the machinery of the Hollywood studio system (including agents, producers, directors and the actor himself) worked to establish what would become Hudson's screen image.

The period between 1948 and 1954 can, in many respects, be regarded as Hudson's apprenticeship as a screen actor. Unlike some of his peers (such as Robert Stack, Natalie Wood, Elizabeth Taylor) Hudson was not a child actor and had almost no prior training as an actor before pursuing a career in cinema. Nor did he come to prominence with a spectacular early performance. His development as an actor was instead gradual and incremental. Hard work and perseverance were the significant drivers of his career development and are also key factors in an understanding of what was to become his star image/persona. The embodiment of the American dream that success might be gained through a strong work ethic, combined with athleticism and clean living, Hudson was to speak very directly to the values of postwar America.

The screen test for Twentieth Century-Fox (1949)

One of the earliest fragments of film to feature the aspiring actor is a screen test for Twentieth Century-Fox made in July 1949, directed by Richard Sale. The test features the twenty-four-year-old Hudson, identified as spending one year at Warner Brothers (during which time he had appeared in *Fighter Squadron*) paired with Kathleen Hughes, a contract player for the studio, notable for her role in low-budget Universal kitsch classics such as *It Came from Outer Space* (1953) and *Cult of the Cobra* (1955). Hughes, who also secured a contract from Universal, would subsequently work with Hudson again on *The Golden Blade* (1953). As with his earlier bit part in *Fighter Squadron*, this footage has assumed a popular legendary status as the epitome of an unsuccessful screen test and, paradoxically, a demonstration that persistence and endeavour can triumph over all, even a deficit of talent. As Sara Davidson notes in *Rock Hudson: His Story*, 'one of the tests is still shown by Twentieth Century-Fox to young actors as an example of how bad one can be and still, through hard work, become a star' (Davidson and Hudson 1986: 45).

The purpose of any screen test is to simultaneously assess an actor's dramatic range, the ability to occupy and move through space and how he or she looks in a range of potential dramatic situations, camera angles, lighting set-ups and arrangements. The scene for the Twentieth Century-Fox test is the lounge of a glamorous apartment. Hudson hurriedly prepares the room and dresses for a rendezvous with Ellie (played by Hughes). He rushes around, preparing the room, drawing attention to his physical stature and his gangly, awkward arms as he moves from the front to the back of the set. He sets out glasses and evidently struggles to uncork a bottle of champagne before rushing to throw on a jacket and answer the door to Ellie. Rather than the suave sophisticate that his handsome features might imply, he appears to be the gauche young man from the midwest that at this point he was. Notably, Raoul Walsh, who was to cast him in several Westerns, had thought that, rather than presenting him as a man of action, this kind of setting and role would suit him better: 'at the time I saw him he was going on the soft side; I suggested he watch Cary Grant' (Moss 2011: 281). While Walsh may well have been correct in the long run, at this point there is little evidence in the frantic and 'action-packed' way that he moves around this sophisticated setting of the urbane man about town. The awkwardness of these opening seconds is further emphasised as his guest arrives. Panting nervously before he even opens the door, he delivers the line, 'Ellie, I knew you'd come back', leaving no time for Hughes to deliver her own response, 'Hello Bick', before he grabs her by the left arm and appears to push her into the room, snatching her coat and purse from her and throwing them onto the couch before pulling at her arm to 'celebrate with champagne'. As the camera pans into a midshot of the couple, an exchange takes place that is the motivation for the scene. Ellie has had to consider her relationship with Bick and he has been anxiously awaiting her return. The scene then places Hudson as the vulnerable partner in this encounter and demands that the actor modulate his performance as our comprehension of the dynamics of their relationship becomes clearer. Moving to the couch and into a medium close-up, Hudson has to turn away from Hughes to deliver a moment of reflection that is designed to suggest Bick's reminiscence of his wartime experience, while the camera zooms into a close-up. This sequence of reverie and emotional unburdening is abruptly disrupted by an unexpected phone call that provokes Ellie's suspicions. Her concerns are then dissipated when the caller is revealed to be from the local delicatessen. The scene closes with an obligatory kiss.

The scene therefore requires a demonstration of a range of emotions and changes in tempo and delivery in the space of just over two minutes, from anticipation and urgency, to reflection and emotional appeal, to suspicion and uncertainty and, finally, to humour and romance. The results of the test undeniably have comedy value (albeit unintentionally). Hudson fumbling with the buttons of his jacket, yanking the hapless Hughes into the room, his lightning change from pensive reverie at his war experience to confessions of love, all inevitably provoke laughter from the modern viewer. Nevertheless, the scene asks a lot of any actor, especially an inexperienced novice such as Hudson. As Andrew Higson notes in an essay on film acting, 'Crucially, what determines the scope of the actor's facial, gestural and corporeal register are the details of framing, angle and distance of shot and focus …' (2004: 153). Given that this is the case, the assessment of Hudson's skills at this stage in his career as meagre or lacking seems to me unduly critical as he demonstrates the capacity to scale his performance according to the constraints of the cinematic frame, a technique that some actors can take a considerable amount of time to perfect. It is quite true to argue that he does not yet occupy space and move with confidence through a scene. However, his ability to respond and to react to another actor's performance is already in evidence. Just as importantly, as Sirk noted, 'the camera sees with its own eye' and the specifics of Hudson's physicality and in particular his adeptness at conveying vulnerability (while simultaneously remaining resolutely masculine) is both an appealing and also a rather unsettling quality

(Halliday 1972: 86). It can scarcely be disputed that he appears clumsy in the early part of the test. In part, at least, this is due to the quite complicated blocking of the scene, demanding a level of nervous activity that then needs to be toned down significantly for the medium close-up dialogue sequences. It is in the more 'romantic' elements of the test that Hudson's potential manifests itself. Notwithstanding the rather hilarious shift between a recollection of war and his profession of love for Ellie (accompanied by a deep intake of breath and rapid turn of the head), Hudson's good looks (filmed in close-up and medium shots), deep yet soft voice and open expression are ideal for the role of the romantic lead. It is in this part of the test that his skill in handling this kind of close camerawork reveals itself. At this early point in his career, Hudson demonstrates performative qualities that transcend his material, doing so even within the context of a screen performance that has often been held up to ridicule.

In *Star Studies: A Critical Guide*, Martin Shingler identifies *photogeny* (i.e. good looks) and *phonogeny* (i.e. a pleasing voice) as far from superficial considerations in an understanding of the qualities that could garner an actor a successful film career. At six feet and four inches in height and with dark wavy hair and classically uniform features, Hudson embodies (as I will discuss in the next chapter) the, albeit clichéd, ideal of the 'tall, dark and handsome' man. Consequently, his physical beauty, which (while culturally and socially specific) has stood the test of time, positions him as an ideal candidate for a pretty diverse range of roles. Shingler also notes that good looks can entail some less positive consequences, observing the 'ambivalences and insecurities of beauty, raising questions about the way in which excessive beauty can be limiting for a film actor in terms of restricting the types of roles they are allowed to play' (2012: 74). Hudson's good looks and his status as 'good scenery' have undeniably often taken attention away from a consideration of his performances in critical accounts. Indeed in his early screen

```
TWENTIETH CENTURY-FOX STOCK TEST

DIRECTOR ..........RICHARD SALE
CAMERA ....................CASTLE
SOUND .......................WARD
DATE ......................7/8/49

              ROCK HUDSON

         HEIGHT ....6'3½"
         WEIGHT ......200
         AGE .........24

BACKGROUND:
1 year at Warner Brothers

SUPPORTED BY: KATHLEEN HUGHES
```

Hudson's famously unsuccessful screen test reveals signs of early promise

appearances he was cast because of his physical attributes rather than anything else. Furthermore, I would argue that Hudson's physical and (perhaps more specifically) his facial beauty has rarely been regarded as contributing in a positive sense to the creation of his performances, with the possible exception of Frankenheimer's *Seconds* (1966). In short, his good looks often conspired against him as far as a critical reputation goes. I think it is also interesting to note that, even while his potential for playing romantic roles was clear even from this early stage, he was in fact rarely cast in such roles at the start of his career. Indeed, as we will see in the second chapter, it is not until this aspect of his range was fully exploited that he was to achieve star status.

The role of the agent: Henry Willson

The years between 1948 and 1954 are also the period during which a group of industry professionals who all made an investment in Hudson as a commodity, worked collectively to shape their actor's image and to identify what he represented. The principal figures in this process of development include the agent Henry Willson, the director Raoul Walsh and latterly the producer Ross Hunter and the director Douglas Sirk, both of whom will be discussed in the subsequent chapters of this book. This period should be understood as the point in Hudson's career when the type of actor he would become and the specifics of his performance style were as yet undecided. Just as importantly, what Hudson represented in terms of a model of masculinity was likewise in a state of flux. This was then the stage of his career when the young actor and those around him were developing the idea of 'Rock Hudson' as an actor and personality and also trying out 'versions' of Rock Hudson on audiences.

Probably the first key player (after Roy Fitzgerald himself) in the process of formulating Hudson's image was the Hollywood agent

Henry Willson, who was what would probably be described as a Hollywood 'insider'. His father had been the president of Columbia Records in New York and the young Willson had moved to the West Coast and started his career as a writer for the *Hollywood Reporter* before becoming an agent for Zeppo Marx in the late 1930s. He came to prominence by launching the career of Lana Turner and worked as a talent scout for David O. Selznick. By the 1940s, Willson had established his own agency, handling the careers of many of the major actors of the time, including Lana Turner, Jennifer Jones, Natalie Wood and Dorothy Lamour. He was also, by the late 1940s and early 50s, operating in an industrial context that was coming to an end. Tom Kemper, in his forensic examination of the emergence of the agent during the 1930s and 40s, has observed that the 50s 'marks the rise of the agents, when corporate agencies were supplanting agencies built around the personality and connections of one or two individuals' (2010: xiii). Willson, who was notoriously ruthless in his own personal ambition and in his endeavours to promote his clients, belonged then to an often nepotistic and increasingly outmoded mechanism for managing and casting actors in productions.

As is almost always the case in the biographies of Hollywood stars, provenance is something of a contested territory and there are at least three versions of how Willson first met the aspiring actor Roy Fitzgerald, who would become Rock Hudson, starting with the story of a chance encounter in the postroom of Selznick Productions where Fitzgerald was a delivery boy. An alternative version suggests that Fitzgerald, working as a truck driver, was much more proactive in making contact with industry professionals; for example, by having professional photosets produced and hanging around studio backlots in the hope that his good looks would be noticed (Hofler 2005). Willson's homosexuality was well known in Hollywood and, although accounts of Willson's and Hudson's past are frequently contradictory and unreliable, it also seems that, at the start of his career, the young actor's homosexuality was not the scrupulously maintained secret it would become just a few years later. Indeed, most accounts seem to suggest that Roy Fitzgerald made use of both his sexuality and his good looks to gain introductions and was a familiar figure in the Hollywood gay milieux.[2]

Whichever version of events is true, Willson quickly identified the young man as enjoying the kind of physical attributes that would entitle him to a place on his growing roster of young male actors. Furthermore, most accounts confirm the importance of Willson's role in the orchestration of Fitzgerald's transformation into a major Hollywood star. This process of course is made manifest by the act of naming and it is Willson (although once again accounts differ) who came up with the name Rock Hudson. Providing names for his clients was something that Willson had a particular instinct for, choosing appellations that seemed particularly attuned to the zeitgeist, names that captured an aura of glamour and (in many cases) sexual allure. So the prosaic Julie Jean Turner was reimagined as the peroxide *femme fatale* Lana Turner. Francis Timothy McCown became Rory Calhoun, the rugged star of Westerns. Calhoun had originally been named Troy Donahue by Willson but this name was destined instead to be bequeathed to Merle Johnson, Jr who, alongside Tab Hunter (*né* Arthur Andrew Gelien), was to become one of the blond heartthrobs of the era. The name Rock (for a short period during 1949 'Roc') Hudson supposedly carried connotations of strength and solidity with its associations to the Rock of Gibraltar and the Hudson River.

Willson arranged for Hudson to take some acting lessons with the drama coach Florence Cunningham and, just as importantly, invested some time and money in addressing his voice, which was, according to Oppenheimer and Vitek, 'thin, high and bore the unmistakable stamp of the Midwest' (Davidson and Hudson 1986: 23). The person charged with addressing this issue was Lester Luther, who Willson had first enlisted as a vocal coach as part of the training programme at Selznick. Luther's voice-training technique was idiosyncratic. Hudson was advised to wait until he had a sore throat or cold and shout as loud as he could. As Davidson informs us, 'This would supposedly break the vocal chords and when they healed the voice would be lower' (Davidson and Hudson 1986: 46). While the efficacy of this strategy may be called into question, there is no trace of the 'thin, high' voice in any of Hudson's screen performances from the first to the last, so we can only assume that Luther's techniques worked.

The beefcake phenomenon

During the course of the 1950s Willson's activities as an agent were to become increasingly associated with an especially successful emergent trend. In almost every respect the caricature of the 1950s, as a period of fixed and unquestioned gender roles, rigid conformity and complacency is, as many scholars have already argued, almost completely false. Steven Cohan, for example, has noted that the decade marked a period in which the male body was increasingly becoming a site for erotic investment in popular culture. Cohan observes that this wider preoccupation with male physicality was literally embodied in the films of the period:

The bodybuilding subculture produced a panoply of erotic male imagery, some of it covert … much of it overt … beefcake spectacle was instantly received on both sides of the Atlantic as celebrations of American masculinity … like the physique photography of the period which supplied the conventions for representing the muscular body on screen. (1997: 182)

One of Willson's 'specialisms' was the identification and subsequent aggressive promotion of young male actors whose qualifications were as much about their good looks and athletic bodies as their dramatic range. The film critic Sidney Skolsky, identifying this trend, was to describe Guy Maddison, one of Willson's protégés as 'beefcake', coining a phrase to denote the male equivalent of 'cheesecake' models and actresses and summing up the appeal of many of Willson's clients and the slew of similarly goodlooking, well-built young men who were to become familiar faces in film (Spoto 1993: 172).

These young men were often promoted by way of photo features showing them off in varying states of undress in the many fan magazines of the period such as *Photoplay*, *Silver Screen*, *Movieland*, *New Movie Magazine* and the UK's *Picture Show*.[3] Indeed beefcake shots became staple fare for the fan magazines from the early 1950s. These images worked in more than one way. They were, for example, often published as a way of introducing 'new faces' to potential moviegoers and thereby functioning in some respects as market research into audience responses to the looks and appeal of a new contract player. Tino Balio notes that contract performers were under strict obligation to undertake whatever marketing the studios deemed appropriate; and that the contract 'gave the studio the right to change an actor's name at its discretion and to control the performer's image and likeness in advertising and publicity', leaving an actor no option but to be photographed however the studio wished (2012: 210). While Willson did not invent the beefcake phenomenon, he was certainly one of the key figures to capitalise on it. This was not least because he was well placed to do so thanks to his growing client list of handsome, fit young actors all sold on the basis of their looks and physiques.

Hudson was no doubt initially regarded as an addition to Willson's coterie, the so-called 'beefcake brigade' and was sold to audiences as another example of the phenomenon. This aspect of his public image was surprisingly long lived, persisting far beyond his early career. Skolsky, for example, was to later identify Hudson as the 'Baron of Beefcake', and the term stuck until the end of his career.

As late as February 1956, by which time he was a fully established star, Hudson appeared in the physique magazine *Tomorrow's Man* alongside Tab Hunter and his close friend George Nader in a feature entitled 'Muscles Make Hollywood Stars'. The admittedly rather flimsy premise of the article is that widescreen cinema had rendered the stuntman largely redundant, and that the new generation of male stars were expected to possess the physicality necessary for action roles, including the ability to perform their own stunts. This is, of course, little more than a pretext to justify the pages of semiclad male flesh on display. What is notable is that, while Hunter and Nader are both pictured engaging in conspicuously 'athletic' activities associated with the cultivation and maintenance of a sculpted physique (swimming, weightlifting and gymnastics), and by so doing in effect 'training' their bodies, by quite marked contrast, Hudson is seen stripped to the waist riding a horse and also using a lumberjack's two-man saw in a forest setting. Hudson's semi-undressed state then is situated in and motivated by physical activities that emphasise his natural and unaffected image, his modesty, his empathy or connection with nature and, by inference, his midwestern, semirural origins. Hudson then is regarded as beefcake but by an accident of nature rather than as the result of a self-conscious design.

Raoul Walsh and Universal Studios

Just as the stories of Henry Willson's first encounter with Hudson are unreliable so, as Marilyn Ann Moss suggests in her study of Raoul Walsh, there are 'conflicting versions' of the way in which the director first met Hudson (2011: 280). This is almost always the case with such stories, especially in an industry that was (and remains) as fuelled by gossip, intrigue and conflict over the provenance of almost any potentially valuable commodity as Hollywood. It seems most likely that Walsh was introduced to the young Roy Fitzgerald by his agent Henry Willson in 1948. Walsh prided himself on his instinctive ability to identify a potential star. Many years before, in the 1930s, he had similarly 'discovered' Marion Morrison, an extra for John Ford, working in the property department at Twentieth Century-Fox. Marion Morrison's conspicuously effete name was changed to John Wayne and he was cast as the lead in *The Big Trail* (1930). Clearly Walsh sensed potential in Hudson too and placed him on a personal contract, working in conjunction with Willson to shape him into a marketable property. This involved continuing vocal and acting lessons with Luther and Cunningham as well as taking guidance on his wardrobe, his hair (which Walsh advised the actor to keep 'long' as it suited casting in Westerns) and paying for dentistry to straighten Hudson's crooked front teeth.

Walsh used a small part in *Fighter Squadron* as an extended screen test for Hudson, who, as I have already mentioned, was to audition for almost all of the major studios in the same period without success. The production context for the film, with Walsh barking instructions at the hapless Hudson, was far from idyllic. In a notable incident, Walsh berated the actor: 'Jesus Christ – you're standing there like a goddamned Christmas tree – get out of the middle of the shot, for Chrissake, or stand sideways so you don't block everybody!' (Moss 2011: 282). It is perhaps surprising then that this awkward atmosphere on set has not translated itself either to the screen or, indeed, to Hudson's proficient if inconspicuous performance in the film. Hudson's role is admittedly minor in terms of dialogue and billing (he is not listed in the cast) and he only appears in several group scenes in recreational settings. While this can hardly be regarded as a *coup de théâtre* for the young actor, it seems unfair to describe his debut in quite the negative terms that have frequently been applied. Even while Walsh was frustrated with this first outing, the director (who was renowned for his lack of patience and tolerance) clearly saw something of note in Hudson and

The eccentric Raoul Walsh

committed to spending more time working with him, eventually in leading roles, as we will see.

Walsh's perspective on Hudson seems to have been a complicated one from the outset. Moss notes that Walsh was to detect something far removed from the fixity and solidity later popularly associated with the actor. Instead:

The one defining word to describe Walsh's feelings about Hudson was ambivalence. He both mentored him and scratched his head about him, for years to come hardly ever moving past that splintered attitude. Hudson was a disturbance to Walsh, something he himself could probably not even articulate. Hudson represented some kind of 'lack,' physically and psychologically. Walsh wanted him to be tough and masculine, something he just couldn't be at that time. All he could do was look handsome, with a body that the camera couldn't help but follow. (2011: 282)

A year after Hudson's inauspicious debut in *Fighter Squadron*, Walsh, according to Sara Davidson, 'sold Rock's contract to Universal International Pictures for $9,000' (1986: 46). This bald statement underlines the nature of power relations between actors and the Hollywood machinery at this point. In effect, the commodity that had been initially shaped and packaged by Walsh and Willson under the name Rock Hudson was sold on to become a contract player for the studio. Danae Clark, in *Negotiating Hollywood: The Cultural Politics of Actors' Labour*, explores in detail the nature of the contractual arrangements between contract players and studios. She notes the power imbalances inherent in studio working practices of this period:

The usual contract ran for seven years, with the studio having the right to take up the option of the actor's services after six months or a year with an increase in pay. If the studio did not take up the option, or wished to fire the actor (with or without stated causes) the contract was terminated. The actor, on the other hand, could not legally break the contract under any circumstances. [...] Since most contracts stipulated that actors must accept the roles 'offered' to them, most actors found themselves playing the same type of role over and over again (1995: 23).

The contract with Universal therefore granted all the rights to Hudson's image and performances to the studio, placing the actor at its complete disposal. While this arrangement seems (and manifestly was) exploitative, the benefits for a novice actor such as Hudson were significant. As a contract player at Universal he underwent a rigorous training programme: he learnt how to ride a horse, dance and fence and was encouraged to exercise to maintain and enhance his athletic physique. He also had acting lessons and was fortunate enough to be taught by the famed acting tutor Sophie Rosenstein, author of *Modern Acting: A Manual* (1936), the head coach at Universal from 1949 until her death in 1952. Rosenstein was one of a generation of women with backgrounds in theatre hired by the studios to train young actors, as noted by Cynthia Baron and Sharon Carnicke (2008: 18–19). Figures such as Phyllis Loughton and Lillian Albertson at Paramount, and Florence Enright, Estelle Harmon and Sophie Rosenstein played a significant role in developing an approach to screen acting and fashioning the performance style of actors within the studios during the 1940s and 50s, not only because of their work as coaches but also because of the acting manuals they wrote based on their methods.[4] Rosenstein had taught drama at the University of Washington before moving to Hollywood to establish an actors' training programme for Warner Bros. in the 1930s. Her approach was intellectually grounded and admirably lucid. As Lisa Sagolla observes, 'Rosenstein wrote in the June 1943 *Warner Club News* "we have only two cardinal principles: 'Absolute sincerity' and 'Absolute simplicity' there is no substitute for genuine emotion"' (2003: 88). Rosenstein's method of study balanced the acquisition of acting skills with a more general education in the arts and social sciences. She advocates in *Modern Acting* that the 'equipment of a trained actor must include […] developed concentration, keen observation, a plastic body, voice and speech adaptability, and a practical knowledge of literature, history, science and the arts' (1936: 3–4). Rosenstein saw the job of the actor to be about 'working from within out, or from the inner feeling to the outward manifestation' (ibid.: 3). This passing remark is not without significance. As we will see in the next chapter, during the mid-1950s Hudson was frequently compared and contrasted in many accounts (sometimes unfavourably) with actors associated with Lee Strasberg and the Actors Studio. We can see very clearly here that Rosenstein, while not a proponent of what was to become popularly known as the 'method', was far from antithetical to Stanislavsky's tenets and Hudson's approach to performance was consequently informed by similar ideas of an imagined interior life realised in a performance.[5] Not only did Rosenstein provide her students with an actor's education inflected by both traditional and perhaps more radical approaches to the craft, she also functioned as a maternal figure for her cohort of young actors. In particular she was to note of Hudson that 'his biggest failing is shyness' but that he 'never had any vanity and was always willing to learn' (Oppenheimer and Vitek 1986: 33).

Hollywood's masculine archetypes

Steven Cohan, in *Masked Men: Masculinity and the Movies in the Fifties* (1997), argues that the years following World War II witnessed what he describes as the middle-class managerial model of masculinity taking hold in American culture and Hollywood cinema. This view is largely corroborated by the work of both Michael Kimmel in *Manhood in America: A Cultural History* (1996) and by James Gilbert in *Men in the Middle: Searching for Masculinity in the 1950s* (2005) and is a subject that will be returned to in the final chapter. This is not to say, however, that the models of virile masculinity produced by Hollywood prior to the 1950s were to be swept away altogether, although Cohan argues that they are increasingly marginalised:

In the fifties, the domesticated breadwinner, commonly identified in the media as *The Man in the Grey Flannel Suit*, was responsible for legitimizing the hegemony of the professional–managerial class. The tough-guy movie hero epitomized by Bogart ... and the Western hero by Wayne ... moved increasingly into the background as a conservative partner in the social consensus. (1997: 38)

Consequently, Hudson's early career and subsequent emergence as a major Hollywood star occurred in an especially dynamic cultural context and coincided with a reconfiguration of models of masculinity and aligned shifts in representations of masculinity. The films under discussion in this chapter then are made at a moment when a period of change (i.e., socially, culturally *and* representationally) in the way that masculinity is figured is starting to take place. This is a point though when older established archetypes that were still prominent in Hollywood cinema were being slowly and incrementally supplanted by newer models. The frontiersman, the soldier, the swashbuckling hero, the lover and the 'boy next door' are all models of masculinity drawn upon by Hollywood, each one becoming entrenched in the vocabulary of popular cinema by the early 1950s. This is, of course, not the entirety of what masculinity meant in America during the 1950s but it can be argued that these are the paradigms of masculinity that are largely enacted during Hudson's film career.[6]

The specific films selected for analysis in this chapter (with the exception of *The Fat Man* [1951]) were all released in 1953 and are illustrative of Hudson's work as he transitions from supporting to featured player.[7] After several years of bit parts and supporting billing, Hudson is beginning to take principal lead in productions and is on the cusp of making an additional leap (as will be seen in the next chapter) from film actor to film star, which indeed happened a year later. The momentum of his career seems to have gained traction in 1953, as evidenced not just by the number and range of productions in which he appeared but also by his increased prominence in film periodicals. The British fan magazine *Picture Show*, for example, illustrates the rapid rise in Hudson's profile during the course of just one year. His name is first mentioned in the magazine on 31 January. In a review for Walsh's *The Lawless Breed*, described as a 'Western Melodrama', Hudson receives a small notice: 'Wes Hardin is finely played by Rock Hudson' (1953: 10). By 4 April, in an issue of the magazine with Doris Day on the cover to promote *April in Paris*, Hudson has become sufficiently recognisable to warrant an autographed, full-page publicity shot on page 7. In the same year, this magazine regularly featured actors ranging from established names to new faces, including Sterling Hayden, Maureen O'Hara, Debbie Reynolds, Mel Ferrer, Michael Denning and Shirley Booth. Only a month later, Hudson was famous enough to warrant cover-star status, with Yvonne de Carlo in a promotional still for *Sea Devils*. Additionally, on page 9, there is an article on *Seminole* and a review on page 10 describes him as 'excellent'. By 14 November, he crops up in the regular competition item 'Match the screen sweethearts and win £20' (1953: 11), alongside major stars Kirk Douglas, Victor Mature, Elizabeth Taylor and Ava Gardner. Finally, in the 5 December issue, a feature on *Back to God's Country* characterises his acting as 'vigorous and good' (1953: 9) and he is the subject of a *Life Story* biographical piece (ibid.: 10). The dizzying range of films that Hudson appeared in during the space of a single year, together with the rapid increase in his profile, vividly demonstrates the extent to which his popularity was building incrementally, even while his identity as a performer and his performance register had yet to be fully determined.

Gun Fury (Raoul Walsh, 1953)

Hudson's first appearance in a Western had been as Young Bull, a native American prepared to kill to get his hands on a gun in Anthony Mann's *Winchester '73* (1950). This was not only a first for Hudson but also for the director, marking Mann's transition from low-budget thrillers to big-budget Westerns, as well as being his first collaboration with his ideal cinematic hero James Stewart. As Basinger notes, 'With *Winchester '73* Mann left film noir behind. It was almost as if he had used the film to conduct his own education in the possibilities of the Western' (2007: 82–3). Hudson was to work again with Mann and Stewart, this time cast in a much bigger role in *Bend of the River* (1952) but it was Raoul Walsh rather than Mann who, in 1953, gave him leading roles in Westerns such as *The Lawless Breed* and (on loan to Columbia Studios) *Gun Fury*.

Raoul Walsh had an exceptionally long career in Hollywood, working as a writer and actor before he started directing and he was to become associated with a range of genres and stars during his fifty years in the business. His oeuvre includes almost all of the popular genres of the early to middle years of the twentieth century from the gangster film to thrillers, war films and swashbucklers. What unifies this diversity of output is his interest in what might best be described as action cinema, as is evidenced in accounts of his working practices. As Lee Marvin, who worked with him on *Gun Fury* was to note:

I don't think he was much interested in dialogue. He was an action director. He loved horses, stagecoaches and explosions. ... If you had a scene to do with dialogue, he'd say, 'You're over here, you're over there, roll it.' Then he'd look down and roll a cigarette and when all this talking had stopped he'd turn to the script girl and say, 'Did they get it all?' She'd say, 'Yeah,' and he'd say, 'Print it.' But for the action stuff he'd get all excited ... Raoul would come to life! (Moss 2011: 332)

Hudson with James Stewart in Anthony
Mann's *Bend of the River* (1952)

Similarly, the cameraman Peter Newbrook recalled that 'his
rehearsals were quite minimal; he would listen to the dialogue and if
he liked what he heard, he would say, "This is a very intelligent
reading. Let's go"' (ibid.: 323).

Although he worked across a range of action genres, it is really
the Western that Walsh is most closely associated with, due in no
small part to his 'discovery' and longstanding collaboration with John
Wayne. This association is also perhaps to do with the stridently
heterosexist values that Walsh personally espoused and frequently
conveyed in fairly unambiguous terms on celluloid. For example,
according to his autobiography, as a young man he had worked as a
cattle herder, after he and his uncle had been shipwrecked on a
journey to Havana. This improbably melodramatic sequence of

events points to Walsh as a prodigious self-dramatist and furthermore as a figure who was romantically attached to the idealism of the frontier and the man of the West who, as Martin Nussbaum notes, writing in 1959,

is the true heroic man, whose characteristics have never varied from Joshua, Ulysses and Lancelot on through the lineage. He is a man with a mission, a faceless man, a universal man of mystery, a 'loner'. And he is a soft-spoken man; for like Joshua, Ulysses and Lancelot he never raises his voice needlessly. But when the action demands, he cries out in anger and righteousness. For example, the Westerner hates guns and killing but he is quick-on-the-trigger when he is compelled to fight. (1959: 461–2)

This particular model of manhood is epitomised by Hudson's role as rancher Ben Warren in *Gun Fury*. The film tells the story of Warren's return home from the civil war on a stagecoach with his fiancée Jennifer Ballard (Donna Reed). Jennifer is kidnapped when the coach is ambushed by a 'notorious' gang led by Frank Slayton (Philip Carey). In the aftermath of this event, the film revolves around Warren's attempt to rally a posse of men to help him rescue his fiancée. At almost every turn his initial struggles to gain assistance are thwarted because no-one is willing to support him (through fear and indifference). His only recourse is to draw on those who hold a grudge against Slayton and his gang, including a reformed gang member, a native American and the Morales girl, Slayton's Mexican lover. The themes of the film are perennial Western concerns: masculine qualities of individual responsibility and agency, the conflict between 'traditional' American values and the nihilism and greed of the criminal gang and, of course, the establishment of explicitly demarcated gender roles and relations. As Stanley Corkin argues, 'the Western, in its specific contours, often appeals to its contemporary viewers in allegorical terms, frequently justifying the culturally dominant activities of a given moment by directly or indirectly locating them as part of a quintessential American legacy' (2000: 67). Additionally, as a film made in the years after the end of World War II, *Gun Fury* engages very clearly with notions of pacifism and the appeal of a retreat into the safety of the homestead, an ideal that Rick Clifton Moore notes is 'shown to be unrealistic' (1996: 107).

Hudson's performance is designed to convey stoicism, a character trait that he would be called upon to demonstrate in many subsequent films, as well as the virile physicality of the Hollywood cowboy. The film is action-packed, with many shootouts and fights, all of which the actor executes convincingly, spending the majority of his time on horseback. As the frontiersman, Hudson is called on to represent a youthful idealism and an indomitability of spirit. For example, in a scene at a town where Warren has been unsuccessful in finding men to join him, he tells the reformed Jess Burgess (Leo Gordon) that, 'A man's gotta do his own growing.'

There is clear evidence here of the actor's efforts to modulate his performance and offer a style of delivery appropriate to the genre. In the action sequences following his fiancée's abduction, for example, he delivers his lines in a staccato fashion, rather than in the softer, measured speech pattern that we are more familiar with, which is reserved for the romantic sequences between Warren and Jennifer at the beginning and end of the movie.

The film is striking both for its spectacular locations and a colour scheme that extends to sets and costumes of greens and terracotta reds that match the landscape perfectly. *Gun Fury* was originally made in 3D and Walsh, who resisted widescreen as an unnecessary development, was a peculiar advocate for this innovation, not least because his vision was not well suited to this new technology, given that he only had sight in one eye. 3D enjoyed only limited success during the 1950s and very few audiences would have seen the film in this format. The major impact of the technology on the production seems to be a recurrence of moments with what seems like rather peculiar and disruptive frontal staging. A particular sequence shows the Morales girl throwing pots and pans in fury at Slayton and then at one of his gang members. The actress is positioned frontally as she performs her assault (for the purposes of 3D filming). However, 'sans technology' we are left instead with a strangely, and unintentionally, Brechtian moment where she appears to address her anger towards the audience.

Sea Devils (Raoul Walsh, 1953)

The swashbuckler, frequently described in contemporaneous literature as 'action melodrama', was still an especially popular genre during the early to middle 1950s. A cursory overview of reviews published in *Picture Show* and *Variety* between 1952 and 1953 indicates the wide appeal of nautical pirate/smuggler-based material or films that reference (however loosely) the exoticism of the Arabian Nights. Other examples of the genre from this period include the pirate adventures *Caribbean Gold* (1952) and *Raiders of the Seven Seas* (1953), an adaptation of *The Prisoner of Zenda* (1952), the Napoleonic adventure *Captain Scarlett* (1953), the Alan Ladd vehicle *Botany Bay* (1953) and the treasure-hunting escapades *Treasure of the Golden Condor* (1953) and *Fair Wind to Java* (1953). Walsh enjoyed considerable success with this kind of material during his long career, notably with *Blackbeard the Pirate* in 1953. *Sea Devils* was inevitably meant to capitalise on these successes rather than break new ground. Even Walsh and his production team considered the script to be 'pretty mundane' (Moss 2011: 324). If nothing else, this was compensated for by beautiful location shooting in the Channel Islands, the film being one of the last Hollywood productions to use the Technicolor three-strip process.

Produced by Coronado and released through RKO, the two leads, Hudson and De Carlo, were on loan from Universal. Hudson, who had played a minor role in *The Desert Hawk* in 1950 (starring

De Carlo), now co-starred with De Carlo, who was a well-known actress by 1953, having established her reputation largely with her performances as 'the Arabian princess of Technicolor forever waiting in Easterns … to be swept off her feet by dark and handsome princes' (Evans 2000: 162). A year earlier, Hudson had appeared in a supporting role as the sea captain Frank Truscott, in pursuit of De Carlo's scheming saloon girl Roxy McClanahan in *Scarlet Angel* (1952). In that film both actors were cast as worldly wise chancers of ambiguous moral standing. The enjoyment for audiences came from the conflict emerging from Truscott's uncovering of Roxy's schemes. *Sea Devils* also offered moviegoers characters whose motives and actions operate at the margins of respectability. Marilyn Ann Moss, in her study of Walsh, summarises the picture by reference to the studio's hyperbolic copy:

RKO's publicity department described the picture as the story of a beautiful heroine named Droucette (De Carlo) who, while on a secret mission, falls in love with a handsome young fisherman-turned-smuggler (Hudson): 'Through his assistance and daring [she] is smuggled from the British Channel Islands into France. Their romance is shattered when subsequent events cause the young seaman to believe Droucette to be a spy for an enemy country. But when her true identity is revealed … they are reunited in a dangerous game of hide-and-seek with death' (2011: 321)

However, the story is much more convoluted than this summary suggests. De Carlo's Droucette is actually a double agent, an English spy who poses as a countess working with the French in a Napoleonic plot to invade England. Perhaps more surprising still, this complex and melodramatic tale is a (very loose) adaptation of Victor Hugo's novel *Toilers of the Sea* (1866). The film begins at sea with Gilliatt (Hudson) aboard his boat *Sea Devil* with fellow smuggler Willie (a young Bryan Forbes). We are informed that war has prevented fishermen from plying their trade, with the result that their only means of income is smuggling. From the outset, therefore, Gilliatt's criminality is motivated by necessity rather than greed. Hudson is costumed in a manner that foregrounds in a rather overdetermined fashion the ways in which we are to understand his role, as is the case in most of these early parts. His hair is windswept, his complexion ruddy. He wears a nineteenth-century cropped and braided nautical-styled jacket and a red neckerchief, matching the red sash around his waist. Forbes is a much smaller man, dressed in a complementary but less well-fitting outfit with the addition of a cap to suggest his status as comic sidekick. Alongside these costume details, the height differential between the two makes Gilliatt appear even more statuesque, the epitome of the nineteenth-century romantic hero. Hudson's performance is broad and self-consciously 'devil may care'. While chased by the coastguard in the opening scene, Gilliatt yells to his apprehensive colleague, 'Smugglers don't sleep, Willie. They fight, get drunk and have a good time!' Unlike the majority of the cast, who are either English or making an approximation of 'Englishness', Hudson makes no attempt at an accent, substituting instead an occasional and rather uncomfortable 'argh' in imitation of the West country burr often associated with sailors, pirates and, naturally enough, smugglers. The role is primarily a physical one, though and Walsh makes considerable use of Hudson's sturdy and naturally athletic physique with several (and often quite gratuitous) scenes with the actor stripped to the waist. Indeed, Hudson is shirtless for almost the entire second half of the film. It is this type of role and this mode of representation that initially earned Hudson the moniker of 'Baron of Beefcake'. However, these kinds of scene are, in fact, infrequent in Hudson's career and it may be their relative scarcity that partly explains their rather overheated reception. This is not to underplay such instances, as the erotic charge of some of these scenes is quite palpable. For example, in one sequence Gilliatt tries to rescue Droucette and is beaten unconscious and captured by his nemesis Rantaine (Maxwell Reed). He is taken below deck and bound around the chest and feet. Hudson is shot in medium close-up in this

The bound Gilliatt (Hudson) artfully presented
for the viewers' delectation in *Sea Devils* (1953),
with Droucette (Yvonne de Carlo)

condition as both Rantaine and Droucette in turn listen to his
explanation for his actions and observe him in captivity. His bound
and naked chest, subservient, recumbent posture, artfully tousled hair,
carefully lit face (drawing attention to the pinkness of his lips and the
clarity of his eyes) make this scene, rather than a moment of jeopardy,
seem curiously and uncomfortably sexy. Walsh's ambiguous attitude
towards his star becomes ever more apparent in this scene, which so
emphatically draws attention to his physical beauty in this rather
eroticised moment. Hudson through his passive and yet stoic posture
and the various aspects of the *mise en scène* (lighting, costume, hair and
make-up) is presented (and presents himself) as an exciting spectacle
of ensnared masculinity.

An earlier tavern scene establishing the romantic charge between Gilliatt and Droucette presents another instance when Walsh's direction highlights both actors' good looks and sex appeal. The scene also and perhaps by accident reveals Hudson's emerging skills as an actor in close-up takes. The sexual tension between the two, already alluded to in their first scene, is emphasised through a complicated, shifting, point of view. In the first half of the scene, we see Gilliatt from Droucette's perspective, watching him as he eats food in a rapacious, manly fashion before fighting with Rantaine. At this point, unaware that he is being watched, Hudson performs an unselfconscious version of the character, physically at ease, sitting carelessly, eating as he sees fit. He is also being objectified in this moment by Droucette's gaze, appearing as an exemplar of 'natural' if brutish, masculinity, first in repose and then in action as he fights. When Gilliatt realises that Droucette is in the tavern and approaches her, the scene shifts to one where she is the subject of attention and Hudson performs as the confident male, buoyed up after his display of aggression, appraising the physical charms of a beautiful woman at the same time as making a deal to transport her to France. The scene is a short one but one that illustrates the technical skills that Hudson is gradually refining in each role. This is a development that is taking place in many respects against the odds as Walsh, as several accounts confirm, was an action director, not especially interested in dialogue sequences. This, together with his notoriety for impatience and a lack of sensitivity, means that Hudson's performances in these early films need to be understood as emerging from what might not be the most conducive or nurturing environment.

The B movie heartthrob

It would be all too tempting in a book that is designed in part to reappraise a maligned actor's performances to focus on films where an actor works with a director whose reputation and status is already well established. Hudson was indeed fortunate that Raoul Walsh took him under his wing and that he was cast in a series of films with the director. He was equally fortunate to work alongside James Stewart, directed by Anthony Mann, and to gain early experience with Douglas Sirk in *Has Anybody Seen My Gal?* (1952). However, for every one of these experiences with directors now regarded as canonical figures of Classical Hollywood, there are just as many examples of less distinguished genre fare, presided over by directors who would scarcely be highly regarded for their authorial vision. The years from 1950 to 1953, after which time he was sufficiently established at Universal to take on leading roles, see him appearing in a succession of minor and walkon parts in various B movies. So, for example, Hudson worked alongside a young Tony Curtis with Charles Lamont (director of many of the Abbot and Costello series of films) on *I Was a Shoplifter* (1950). He also played minor roles in several films directed by William Castle, the notorious director of kitsch horror titles such as *The Tingler* (1959) and *Strait-jacket* (1964). However, even in this kind of B-movie fare, there are examples of Hudson's early performances which offer surprising indicators of promise.

The Fat Man (William Castle, 1951)

Castle gave Hudson an early opportunity to play a more significant role in *The Fat Man*, a film noir based on a successful radio series of the period that was in turn based on the characters of Dashiell Hammett. The radio show was to come to an end when Hammett fell foul of the Hearings on Un-American Activities and was listed in *Red Channels: The Report of Communist Influence in Radio and Television* (1950). So, in part, this cinematic adaptation was a last-ditch attempt to capitalise on the radio programme's prior success

(Dunning 1998: 242). The fat man of the title is Brad Runyan, a private detective (played on radio and on screen by J. Scott Smart), who is called on to investigate the murder of a dentist who seems to have been killed for nothing more than some dental x-rays. The dentist's assistant Jane Adams (Jayne Meadows) asks for Runyan's help in uncovering the true identity of a mysterious client, Roy Clark (Hudson), who is not as he first appears to be.

It's important to note here that during this period of apprenticeship, Hudson frequently took on minor roles atypical to those later associated with him. For example, in *The Fat Man*, he is a petty crook with a past, who eventually comes to a sticky end. In some respects, this part serendipitously parallels the trajectory of Hudson's early career, as he plays a naïve but ambitious young man who invents a new identity for himself to cover up his past, assuming different personas and guises without anyone knowing who he really is.

We are first introduced to the enigmatic Roy Clark in flashback, arriving unexpectedly at the surgery for emergency dental work. In the scene, Roy seems unkempt, casually dressed, flustered and in pain. He does not have enough money to pay for his treatment in full and says he will return a week later. On the next occasion, both appearance and demeanour are very different. The lack of composure that Hudson performs in the first scene is contrasted with a new suavely dressed and composed Roy. Jane recalls this strange change in personality, one that is emphasised and made manifest by a similarly marked change in costume. She also notices that he leaves in a chauffeur-driven car. His status shift is indicated by his change of residency from Wilson's Motel to Sunset 33298, as well as by his use of enthusiastic expressions like 'swell', combining to suggest that in a short space of time this young man's prospects have altered significantly.

The film then becomes a hunt for Roy, a character only ever encountered by the audience in flashback. This inevitably creates a rather heightened and dreamy aura around Hudson's appearance in the film and requires shifts in register from scene to scene and, in some cases, within a single scene, which all make significant demands on the actor's range. (The narrative structure here is blatantly derivative and calls to mind Preminger's 1944 film noir *Laura*, in which Gene Tierney's eponymous character is remembered by separate characters in different ways.) Runyan's trail leads him to Pat Boyd, a nightclub hostess (Julie London) who has also encountered Roy Clark. She recalls that Roy dispensed with a troublesome drunk who was bothering her in a bar she worked in. Alternately efficient in his displays of physical aggression towards the drunk and then coldly taciturn towards Pat, Hudson portrays Roy as the typically jaded and cynical antihero of film noir. To emphasise this, he arrives late for a date in a subsequent scene, by which time we are to understand that Pat and Roy are in a relationship. When Pat expresses her frustration, he tells her, in an emotionless close-up, 'Look baby there's no strings on me. I do what I like and the same goes for you.' This scene demands an emotional arc encompassing anger, hostility and pent-up frustration relieved by romance. Therefore, after their confrontation, when Pat complains that she knows nothing about him, Roy eventually gives her his number and, instead of spending the planned evening at a nightclub, they enjoy a romantic dance in front of a jukebox. This denouement, which presumably is meant to appear charged with sexuality (London seductively removes her coat while Hudson looks on in silent appraisal of her beauty), instead seems touching due to Hudson's obvious youth and his still rather callow physicality. As London joins him for their scene of implied passion, his embrace lacks many of the elements of stylised Hollywood romance. He appears a little clumsy and childlike rather than the polished seducer. Swaying slowly from foot to foot to the music from the jukebox and towering over London, his arms pull her into an embrace that is reminiscent of teenage sweethearts at a prom rather than an act of seduction between two streetwise characters. The next scene, 'that Sunday when we went to the Zoo', is designed to uncover Roy's psychological motivations, affording Hudson the opportunity to hone skills that we have seen him trying out with mixed results before. In a sequence that recalls Hudson's close-up soliloquy in his screen test for Twentieth Century-Fox a year earlier, Roy reminisces about his childhood 'back East', remembering his dreams of escape. This scene calls for a demonstration of a combination of world-weariness and inner sensitivity. Played in close-up, Hudson is frequently shot in profile, his eyes averted from his partner when he moves his head to face her. When she advises him that anybody who wants to can get off the 'dirty street', his smile is nothing more than a cynical upturning of one corner of his mouth. As the scene comes to an end and the couple walk out, arm in arm, Pat tells him: 'You're a funny one. You have more moods than anyone I ever knew' and, based on the evidence here, it does indeed seem that, in a very short period of time, Hudson has progressed from an ingénu with little more than an instinctive sense of technique to a developing actor able to assume a role and suggest interiority. We subsequently learn that Pat and Roy get married and he reveals to his bride that he has a hidden past, involving time spent in jail. Runyan pursues the story of Roy (whose alias is Ray) to a circus and interviews the clown Ed Deets (played by famed clown Emmett Kelly) who remembers Roy/Ray as his cellmate and a stagehand during his time in prison. We discover that Roy was embroiled in an armed robbery disguised as a policeman and that he has been killed by a criminal gang for demanding payment after years of incarceration. Throughout the film we only access Roy through the recollections of others, so he remains a distant and enigmatic figure. This is highlighted not only by elements of his performance but also by the film's narrative construction. As I will argue later, this sense of detachment and distance, hinted at in this low-budget production was to become a recurrent feature of Hudson's subsequent performances.

The Golden Blade (Nathan Juran, 1953)

The Golden Blade (1953) was directed by Nathan Juran, another director of low-budget kitsch cinema, whose films have become objects of camp appreciation, notably, *The Deadly Mantis* (1957), *20 Million Miles to Earth* (1957) and, most famously, *Attack of the 50 Foot Woman* (1958). He was also the director of the Ray Harryhausen extravaganza *The Seventh Voyage of Sinbad* (1958) and *The Golden Blade* was no doubt partly a preparation for the exoticism and spectacle of this later success. This film is an example of another category of swashbuckling adventure that retained its popularity during the 1940s and into the 50s; that is the 'oriental swashbuckler', which, according to Jeffrey Richards was also known colloquially in the industry at that time as the 'tits and sand film' (1977: 270). In the 1940s, Universal had specialised in this kind of material, with movies like Walter Wanger's *Arabian Nights* (1942) and Arthur Lubin's *Ali Baba and the Forty Thieves* (1944). The sets for these lavish (and expensive) productions were put to pragmatic good use in the 1950s by the studio with low-budget productions of the sort that Hudson featured in. In *The Golden Blade*, the actor graduated to top billing after playing second fiddle to Yvonne De Carlo in *Sea Devils* and Donna Reed in *Gun Fury*. *The Golden Blade* definitively accords Hudson priority, with Piper Laurie (who he had worked with a year previously on Sirk's *Has Anybody Seen My Gal?*) in a supporting co-star role.

Hudson had already appeared in a similar production in 1950, in the minor part of Captain Ras in *The Desert Hawk*, directed by Frederick de Cordova, another film-maker associated with low-budget genre films. (De Cordova is perhaps best known as the director of the *Bonzo the Chimp* [1951–2] comedies starring a young Ronald Reagan.) *The Desert Hawk* was not only the first time that Hudson worked alongside Yvonne De Carlo but the film was also photographed by Russell Metty, Sirk's cinematographer of choice in the 1950s. Both films are set in an imagined 'historical' Baghdad that loosely references the exoticism of the *Arabian Nights*. So De Carlo's character in *The Desert Hawk* is called Scheherazade, with Jackie Gleason and Joe Besser playing Aladdin and Sinbad, though these names seem to have little to do with the stories or characters for which they are better known. In *The Desert Hawk*, Hudson is a turban-clad, deeply tanned and bearded authority figure, the captain of the evil Prince Murad's guards. The part requires the physical skills of horse riding and fencing that he was developing as a contract player at Universal. In terms of a specific performance style, the small role makes little demand on him as it is largely a caricature of the pantomime villain. Consequently, he has to do little more than appear stern and impassive and to interrogate tribesmen about the whereabouts of the elusive Omar (the Desert Hawk of the title).

By contrast, *The Golden Blade*, released three years later, provided Hudson with a starring role and therefore required much more from him than the cape-swirling villainy of Captain Ras. Although set once again in Baghdad, *The Golden Blade* is a curiosity, an odd amalgam of narrative themes, drawing on elements of *Arabian Nights*-style adventure and drama, Arthurian legend and, perhaps most jarringly of all, screwball comedy. (It was also the last film of this kind that Hudson was to be involved in, marking an end point in the first stage of his career.) While undoubtedly an odd (some might say incoherent) pastiche of narrative tropes, *The Golden Blade* vividly illustrates Joseph Campbell's monomyth or 'hero's journey', as described in *The Hero with a Thousand Faces* (1949). The film tells the story of Harun (Hudson), who travels from Basra to Baghdad in order to avenge the death of his father. Arriving in the city, Harun meets both a Greek shopkeeper, Barcus (Steven Geray), and the Princess Khairuzan (Piper Laurie), who disguises herself as a commoner to escape the stifling atmosphere of palace life. Harun finds a sword with supernatural powers in the Greek's shop and the film becomes an adventure organised around the substitution and theft of the weapon and the journey to recover and restore it to its destined owner, Harun. In the course of this adventure, Harun and the Princess become romantically linked. A plot to murder both the Princess and her father by the evil Jafar (George Macready) is uncovered and Harun, after recovering the sword (pulled from a stone in the manner of King Arthur), is confirmed as the rightful owner of the Sword of Damascus and his identity is revealed as 'He Who Follows the Righteous Path'.

The Golden Blade draws on what can be seen as recognisable narrative and stylistic tropes. The characterisation and marking out of gendered and social roles is formulaic in the extreme and the dialogue is written in a portentous, faux-antique manner, designed to imitate the ornate phraseology of *Arabian Nights*. In short, the film is a lighthearted swashbuckler and is in no way intended to be taken seriously. It does, however, demand that its cast shift between dramatic registers with some degree of fluidity, moving as it does between moments of action adventure, quasi-mythological fantasy and slapstick comedy. By this stage, Hudson had developed sufficiently as an actor to be able to perform as a swashbuckling hero with much more confidence, even in a low-budget production such as this. For example, in the scene in which he first encounters the Sword of Damascus in Barcus's shop, his physicality as he moves through the shop looking for clothes and equipment suggests dynamism and energy. In medium close-up, he extracts the sword from a pile of fabric, throws it to one side and then appears to have second thoughts. Facing the audience with the activity of the bazaar behind him, he pulls the sword from its sheath, excitement and determination on his face as he appraises the weapon, turning it at angles to assess its blade. This fragment of cinema recalls the dynamic, coiled-spring physicality of Douglas Fairbanks or Errol Flynn, which Hudson seems to have drawn upon. This is not surprising as actors such as Flynn and Fairbanks would have been

Harun (Hudson) uncovers the 'Sword of
Damascus' in the oriental swashbuckler
The Golden Blade (1953)

regarded as the reference points for this particular style of
performance. Similarly, in the many fight sequences, Hudson
(for once) seems to have been able to embody the fleetness of
foot necessary to render them thrilling and fast-paced.

The comedy elements are largely confined to sequences
involving the shopkeeper, Barcus, and Piper Laurie's Khairuzan.
Laurie had already featured in two similar films to this alongside
Tony Curtis, *The Prince Who Was a Thief* (1951) and *Son of Ali Baba*
(1952). *The Golden Blade* in some respects calls on her to reprise
these roles, as well as her parts in *Has Anybody Seen My Gal?* and *No
Room for the Groom* (1951). In the latter she portrays a vivacious and
impetuous young woman, who is headstrong and, consequently,
according to the orthodoxies of Hollywood cinema at least, likely to

get into trouble at any given moment. Laurie had by now marked herself out as an adept light-comedy actor and this film capitalises on this to great effect, playing up her 'tomboyish' and 'fiery' personality, as well as her ability to play physical comedy with a lightness of touch, evidenced in a sequence in which she has disguised herself as a man in a ridiculous hat and robe. Hudson's aptitude for comedy becomes apparent when he is cast alongside someone already well versed in the style. Sharing a ride on the back of Hudson's horse, Khairuzan, in her 'masculine' disguise, quizzes Harun about his motivations. Midway through the journey, Harun becomes exasperated with his passenger and suggests 'he' (Khairuzan) should be horsewhipped. As if to convey a mixture of fear and perhaps excitement, Laurie leans forward and grasps Hudson's chest asking, 'What would you do with me?' Hudson then looks confused by this unmanly embrace and turns his head downwards. In close-up, a point-of-view shot shows the Princess's bejewelled slipper and Harun realises he has been duped. Hudson continues to deliver his lines but his slight smile and change in demeanour indicate to us that he now knows his 'male' companion to be an imposter. He smiles, laughs and responds, 'I do not know … yet.' And with this, the scene ends.

The Golden Blade is a minor film and I would not wish to claim that it should be regarded otherwise. Indeed Hudson himself, often deprecating about his own work, described it as 'a terrible movie I've made with Piper Laurie' (Oppenheimer and Vitek, 1996: 65). Laurie was to recall that, during that period, 'He never felt any of his work was any good' (ibid.: 36). Yet his performance in this film illustrates very well the journey that Hudson had taken in a short space of time, from an inexperienced, awkward and self-conscious performer to a versatile, energetic actor with the screen presence and dramatic range to carry a film. Far from the one-dimensional account of the 'wooden' but handsome 'Baron of Beefcake', to borrow Skolsky's term, we can see instead a career built around hard work, perseverance and an undeniable (but difficult-to-define) screen presence. These qualities are the necessary characteristics for any successful screen actor and in Hudson's case the groundwork had been done by the end of 1953. During the next stage of his career (and in an even shorter timeframe), he became one of the biggest Hollywood stars of the 1950s.

2 THE TALL, DARK AND HANDSOME STAR

By the end of 1953 Rock Hudson had appeared (credited and uncredited) in twenty-seven films. He had worked across a range of genres including thrillers, Westerns, swashbucklers and comedies, with a variety of directors, from the well-known and respected Anthony Mann and Raoul Walsh to jobbing figures such as Sidney Salkow and William Castle. He had developed a craft and an emergent style as a stoic but sensitive, potential romantic lead and he was repeatedly described by colleagues and the popular press as a 'hardworking' actor. Nonetheless, fellow contract player Piper Laurie told Oppenheimer and Vitek in the biography *Idol* that Hudson's good looks and athletic build did not initially bring the success that Universal's executives might have hoped for and that 'it was obvious to everyone that Rock's career was not taking off in the same way Tony Curtis's was … Rock came perilously close to being dropped by the studio' (1986: 36).

What was needed by the middle of the 1950s to sustain his career and to justify the initial investment by Henry Willson and Raoul Walsh (and subsequently by Universal) was a commercial success to shift Hudson from the status of contract player to that of a fully fledged star. In 1954 this happened with the release of *Magnificent Obsession*, a film that was, as the standard account of his career has it, to 'catapult' him to stardom. There can be little doubt that this film resituated Hudson within Hollywood. No longer a supporting player in low-budget releases, henceforth he would become one of the most recognisable and popular actors in cinema for the rest of the decade and beyond. As Barbara Klinger observes,

He was voted the most popular male movie star by *Modern Screen* in 1954, *Look* in 1955, *Photoplay* in 1957, and by theatre owners the same year. From 1957 to 1964 the Film Buyers of the Motion Picture Industry consistently named him the number one box office attraction, which meant that audiences bought more tickets for his movies than anyone else's … . Hudson was unquestionably the strongest box office attraction Universal had from the mid-1950s through the early 1960s and arguably the most popular male star of the time overall. (1994: 99)

The conditions for this sustained popular success were provided, in part at least, by a second group of industry professionals who invested their own careers and energies in the construction and maintenance of Hudson's star persona. Just as at the start of his career Willson and Walsh had collaborated to develop the image and acting skills of the young Roy Fitzgerald, so in the mid-1950s Willson was to be joined (and ultimately supplanted) by figures at Universal, principally the producer Ross Hunter and the director Douglas Sirk. These individuals were most evidently responsible for fashioning the image, roles and performances that were to define Rock Hudson as a star. Rather than the frenetic testing out of roles and types that might suit the young actor, which characterised the early years of his career, it is from this point that his public image and his dramatic range become fixed. In short, Rock Hudson the film star emerges.

Barbara Klinger, in a chapter devoted to the popular reception of Hudson in both the 1950s and 80s in her book *Melodrama and Meaning: History, Culture and the Films of Douglas Sirk*, equates Hudson's importance as a cultural icon with the fact that he 'embodied a certain brand of sexual normalcy' (ibid.). For Klinger,

Hudson functioned as the epitome of American ideals of masculinity, 'a strapping, physically appealing, clean cut, often sensitive, and ultimately morally upright character' (ibid.: 100). As we will see in this chapter, the construction of Hudson's star image was achieved through casting choices and performances within key films, reinforced by promotional materials that can be situated within a wider set of debates taking place during the period. In particular, his star status is established around what might be described as his representative quality, in effect his ability to summon up an ideal of stability and (to use Klinger's terminology) 'normalcy' that, as I will argue later on, is more ambivalent than it might at first appear. This is played out in a series of films in which he is cast in roles that illustrate, as Paula Black has observed in her work on 1950s advertising, the two exemplars of 'modern' masculinity during the decade: the romantic man (the primary focus of this chapter) and the military hero, mentioned at the end of the chapter (2004: 36–7). My argument here is that these two parallel models of masculinity provide the basis on which Hudson's stardom was to be constructed but that the significance as well as the performance of these idealised archetypes is ambiguous, complicated and precarious in many instances. Furthermore, in this chapter I am suggesting that the image construction initiated by Henry Willson and Raoul Walsh was to be taken up by two further industry figures, whose job was to shape Rock Hudson as Universal's leading male star. In particular, in this chapter the refinement of Hudson's performance style is linked to discussion of film acting more generally, specifically the contemporaneous emergence of the 'method'.

Ross Hunter and Douglas Sirk

During the middle of the 1950s, initially due to a succession of commercial hits with Douglas Sirk, Ross Hunter was to become a major Hollywood producer, recognised for his lavishly mounted productions. As Bernard Dick notes, 'he was dubbed the producer with the Midas touch … Hunter agreed that style was meaning but style also meant money. He was so successful at translating elegance into profits that other studios were soon courting him' (1997: 154). Robert Hofler summarises the Hunter style, drawing on one of his most notorious maxims:

His formula was as pure as it was absurd: beautiful actors, beautiful costumes, beautiful sins. As he put it, 'You might just as well have a murder take place on an antique Oriental rug as on someone's dirty linoleum.' (2005: 235)

This caricature of Hunter as a cynical purveyor of populist trash (a characterisation that Hunter himself was consistently complicit in reproducing) tends to underplay his industrial significance. Hunter possessed sound financial management skills and also a knack for innovation.[1] For example, in 1964 *Life* magazine ran an article discussing the use of title sequences and their increased creativity and length. In this feature, Hunter is singled out for particular mention for his product-placement strategies:

Producer Ross Hunter, whose highly styled films have endeared him to fashion leaders, has discovered that furriers, jewellers, fashion houses and manufacturers will let him have no end of their wares in return for a simple screen credit. 'I use my titles to save money,' Hunter says. (1964: 103)

In short, by the mid-1950s, Hunter's films not only kept Universal afloat but also facilitated a shift in the studio's reputation. No longer just responsible for low-budget horror and science fiction, Universal was to become associated with popular and luxurious 'adult' productions. Hunter's commercial instincts for what would appeal to audiences were to sustain him throughout his career and were frequently nostalgic in tone, referring back to what he saw as the glory days of Hollywood glamour during the 1930s. This inevitably meant that remakes of popular films from the 1930s became a Hunter speciality, appealing to both his shrewd business sense as well as to his more romantic inclinations. It is also no minor biographical detail that Hunter was gay and lived and worked with his long-time partner, the production designer Jacques Mapes during the height of his successes in Hollywood. He was consequently then an acquaintance (though reputedly not a friend) of Henry Willson and also familiar with Hudson who, by this time was not only Willson's client and a Universal contract player but a regular face in the gay nightlife of Hollywood. While accounts (inevitably) differ, it does seem that Hunter had Hudson very clearly in mind as a lead contender for the role of reformed playboy Bob Merrick in *Magnificent Obsession* and, alongside Douglas Sirk, he was subsequently to enthusiastically embrace the task of creating the actor's star image.

Douglas Sirk's work during his tenure at Universal Studios has received a great deal of academic attention, with several of his films now widely regarded as a subversive critique of post-war American society, hidden beneath the glossy surfaces of romantic and seemingly banal dramas, termed 'family melodrama' in Thomas Elsaesser's foundational essay 'Tales of Sound and Fury'.[2] This reputation as a 'subversive auteur' is due in no small part to the director's own ability to critically situate his work, which was to come to the fore in a succession of interviews after his retirement, first for *Cahiers du cinéma* in the mid-1960s and subsequently with Jon Halliday in the early 70s, forming the basis of the book *Sirk on Sirk: Conversations with Jon Halliday*. It is not my intention to revisit this significant body of literature, which has been discussed exhaustively elsewhere.[3] What matters for the purposes of this study is Sirk's role in the development of Hudson as both an actor and as Universal's leading male star from the mid-1950s onwards. Sirk was to recount his role in this process in the Halliday interviews. First, he was to

Hudson, Douglas Sirk, Jane Wyman and Ross
Hunter (*Magnificent Obsession*)

imply that he 'discovered' Hudson after seeing him in a small part in
the B movie boxing drama *Iron Man* (1951). Sirk claimed that a
meeting was arranged on the basis of this film, which then resulted in
a lengthy screen test and, ultimately, to Hudson being cast in *Has
Anybody Seen My Gal?* in 1952. Sirk's attitude towards Hudson was
at points contradictory (not unlike Walsh's in the early 1950s) and in
all respects reflective of his own wider disenchantment with the
commercialised sector of the film industry where he found himself
working during his years at Universal. His attitude towards Hudson's
homosexuality is also revealing. He suggests, in *Sirk on Sirk*, that
Ross Hunter somehow 'made' Hudson gay:

I sometimes think Ross Hunter played a part in pushing Rock towards being
homosexual. At first Rock seemed to me to lie near the middle of the sexual

spectrum, but when he met Ross, that was it. The studio had a heck of a time trying to hide Rock's homosexuality. (1997: 107)[4]

On balance, Sirk's assessment of Hudson was simultaneously paternalistic and cynical, describing him as a handsome, endearing personality but also as naïve and childlike. In an interview with Michael Stern collected in *Action!* (Morris 2009), he says:

Rock Hudson was not an educated man, but that very beautiful body of his was putty in my hands. And there was a certain dialectic at work in his casting, especially after *Magnificent Obsession*. This film he did not understand at all. But after it I used him as a straight, good looking American guy. A little confused, but well meaning. (2009: 28–9)

Sirk then was a key figure in moulding Hudson's star image but as a director was motivated to cast him for what might be regarded as strategic purposes. He was interested in Hudson, not for his charisma or his star quality but instead for his 'typicality' or his representative value. In essence, what mattered to Sirk was the particularly American ideals and sets of associations that Hudson seemed to embody and this subsequently informs both his approach to directing him and the performances that emerge from that process.

Albert Zugsmith, who produced both Sirk's *Written on the Wind* (1956) and *The Tarnished Angels* (1957), remarked on the director's working practices. Zugsmith regarded Sirk as exacting and austere in his approach to staging and filming productions, in other words, as a technician:

There was no improvisation, none whatsoever, on the part of the actors in these films. There were conferences, meetings, quasi-rehearsals. Improvisation was unnecessary. Sirk worked very closely with the camera man placing the shots himself. In this respect he was similar to Orson Welles. Metty was an excellent camera man. (ibid.: 36)

Actors on Sirk productions then were given especially rigorous direction and expected to perform in very precise ways within what James Naremore has termed a meticulously composed and organised 'performance frame'.[5] This additionally illustrates the extent to which, across the course of eight films,[6] Hudson had to forge a new and very much more disciplined working practice with a director who demanded rigor in the execution of his stylistic vision and this extended to what he wanted his actors to do on screen. Hudson had already proven himself an actor eager to develop his skills and learn his 'craft' in his early career, and now, with Sirk, he was to show that he could respond to precise direction. For Sirk, Hudson represented an archetypical all American model of masculinity and, as an actor, he offered the director malleable raw material that could be shaped to suit his purposes.

My argument in this book is that Hudson's performances cannot be meaningfully understood in isolation as examples of film acting in and of themselves. Instead I am suggesting that we might better understand and read Hudson both as actor and film star through a set of (what I am describing here for the sake of clarity as) interpretive *filters* or *lenses*. These lenses, provided by a range of individuals involved in the development of his style and career, contextualise his performances. This is, of course, to a greater or lesser degree true of any actor but my contention is that, in this case, a specific constellation of industry figures yields very particular and remarkable results in Hudson's studied composure.

The first (and perhaps most significant) lens through which we can read Hudson's performances is that of the actor himself: Roy Fitzgerald, a gay man from a provincial midwestern background in Illinois, who brings to bear his culturally determined and socially located ideas of masculinity. He served in the navy during World War II and worked as a truck driver following the war. Fitzgerald's life from the outset was about performing a sanctioned notion of heterosexual masculinity. The second lens through which to understand Hudson's performances is that of his agent Henry Willson, who was instrumental not only in 'discovering' the actor but also in managing his client's image. Willson was a gay man marketing male actors chosen for their good looks and athletic bodies. His clients were sold to audiences on the basis of their sex appeal and, consequently, their images, film roles and even names were constructed to convey a sexualised and commodified masculinity. Third, Hudson's image and performances have to be read through the filter of Raoul Walsh's influence. Walsh's own resolutely masculine persona was an invention (or perhaps, more accurately, a reinvention) emerging from his own vivid imagination. The director was obsessed with the drama of an unproblematic and unquestioning macho masculinity and had been central to the creation of some of the key masculine icons of Hollywood cinema. Walsh had imagined Hudson as the new edition to this pantheon of 'real' men. The fourth lens through which we can decipher Hudson is that of producer Ross Hunter. Universal's producer with the 'Midas touch', Hunter's love of the glamour, excess and romance of 1930s Hollywood resulted in an ambition to resuscitate the dream factory by producing films with beautiful sets and beautiful actors in the face of what he regarded as a rather less appealing investment in realism. Key to these dreams of glamour were the romantic lead actors and actresses who could function as role models. Tall, dark and handsome, Hudson's looks and image almost perfectly reflect the values that Hunter was to sell to audiences with great success. The final lens through which we can interpret Hudson's performances from the mid-1950s onwards is that of Douglas Sirk, an intellectual European film director and one with a rather cynical attitude both towards his subject matter and the Hollywood industry. Sirk's films at various points seem to either celebrate American values (including gender roles and norms) or critique and undermine them. In Hudson, he found an actor who appeared to be the epitome of the all American boy next door and consequently the perfect vehicle through which to begin to question (albeit subversively) that very ideal.

This very particular conjunction of individuals who were all (to a greater or lesser degree) involved with the production of models of masculinity (at the level of performance and/or representation) inevitably complicates any reading of Hudson's star image and performance style. Far from 'straightforward' and 'uncomplicated' (the adjectives often used in reviews and critical accounts of his roles), the constructions of masculinity enacted by Hudson carry a burden of expectation and fantasy. In the figure of Rock Hudson, we can see an accretion of associations, interpretations and 'versions' of masculinity that were initially established in the early 1950s, refined during the mid-50s (the period that is the primary focus in this chapter) and played out and, ultimately, unpicked during the rest of his career.

Sirk was to claim that the success of his Universal melodramas hinged on the ways in which stories were strategically constructed around what he described as 'split' or 'in-between' characters, alongside characters whom he regarded as 'immovable':

In melodrama it's important to have one immovable character against which you can put your more split ones. Because your audience needs – or likes – to have a character in the movie that they can identify themselves with: naturally the steadfast one, not to be moved. (1997: 112–13)

The director contended that he consciously used Hudson as this 'steadfast' point of reference. However, we should note that Sirk's reading of his output during the Universal years tends to be revisionist. In effect, Sirk is rereading his own films in the light of the *Cahiers du cinéma* interview in 1967 and subsequent accounts of his importance (including his own observations) become interpretations that are open to question.[7] I would argue that Hudson's casting, performance and star signification produce far more than uncomplicated steadfast figures of identification across this period, not least in his films for Sirk. So, instead of Sirk's simplistic formulation of Hudson performing as a 'regular guy' that has tended to be reproduced in popular accounts fairly unquestioningly, I am arguing that his performances across the films that were to establish his star status are better understood as representations of a certain type of stoicism, one that is frequently distanced and alienated (as we will see in several of the case studies to follow) or, alternatively, portrayals of, what I am describing here as, the 'changed man'.

Narratives of redemption are central to the storytelling strategies deployed within Classical Hollywood cinema, even at this late stage. Hudson was frequently cast as someone who realises the errors of his ways and in the process is reformed. So, the dissolute playboy in *Magnificent Obsession*, Bob Merrick, progresses through the narrative from purposelessness to purposefulness. His story becomes one of a man who, through a sequence of improbable circumstances, moves from a recognisably 'unacceptable' model of masculinity (the feckless playboy and libertine) to a socially sanctioned and conformist model (the medical professional). When Hudson is cast as one of Sirk's supposedly immovable figures, he is often positioned as distant, diegetically (as a marginal or marginalised character, for example) and visually, due to his placement within the *mise en scène*. This means that he often plays someone at the periphery, or not fully embedded, in the world in which he finds himself. So rather than being a point of identification for an audience, he seems to be a liminal figure, one placed in the narrative to observe the foibles and contradictions of the other characters. This liminal quality often extends itself to an acting style that can at points seem pensive and detached, contributing a certain enigmatic quality to his performances across many of his most successful films. Interestingly, the liminality of Hudson's position within the narratives of many of the films under discussion here becomes one of the recurrent characteristics of the roles that he was to take on in the years to follow.

Magnificent Obsession (Douglas Sirk, 1954)

Typically, accounts of the production context for *Magnificent Obsession* vary depending on the source. By 1953–4 Douglas Sirk had worked with Hudson on both the light comedy *Has Anybody Seen My Gal?* and the Western *Taza, Son of Cochise* (1954). However, Sirk did not seem to have been especially invested in Hudson's career at this point, as he was to tell Jon Halliday that it was Ross Hunter's enthusiasm both for a remake of *Magnificent Obsession*, with Jane Wyman (on loan from Warners Bros.) in the starring role, and for a young contract player called Rock Hudson, that got him involved (against his better instincts) in the project. The original film version had been a major success for Universal in 1935 and Sirk suggested that it was Wyman's interest in a remake, which finally persuaded him to take the project on. Sirk also claimed, as I have previously noted, that Hunter 'was very keen on promoting Rock Hudson who was then just a beginner in Hollywood' (1997: 107). Ironically, this 'beginner' had already made nearly thirty films. Jane Wyman's version of events is rather different.[8] Wyman, a major star at Warners, with an Oscar and two Golden Globes to her name, claims that she was shown a series of potential co-stars (probably by Ross Hunter) and that, after watching an unspecified Western, she chose Rock Hudson to be her leading man. The actress suggested that her conviction that he was the right actor led him to be cast on that basis, going straight into wardrobe without so much as a screen test. Hudson's own account of proceedings differs yet again and, on balance, seems like the most persuasive version. Hudson remembered going through an extensive testing process, which was usual for Sirk, who had done the same prior to casting him in *Has Anybody Seen My Gal?*. According to Hudson, Sirk 'asked Rock to do eight scenes – two days of extensive testing, then looked at the film with his producer Ross Hunter. They decided Rock was ready to handle the starring role' (Davidson 1986: 71).

However contradictory the stories, there is no question that Jane Wyman was *the* major star of the production, as vividly illustrated by its budget. As a star on loan from another studio, Warner Brothers was able to determine its price for her services, with the result that a fee of $150,000, a sizeable percentage of the film's $780,000 budget was dedicated to her salary.[9]

Being cast as co-star to Jane Wyman in any film was a significant step change in Hudson's career and his industry profile. Like Hudson's, Wyman's career had been built through hard work and perseverance. Her background was similarly undistinguished and she had arrived in Hollywood from the midwest (Missouri) in the 1930s to work as a chorus girl in a succession of musicals. Graduating from uncredited parts to become a contract player (frequently seen in comedies), she was cast as Ray Milland's girlfriend in Billy Wilder's *The Lost Weekend* (1945), gaining positive reviews that expressed some degree of surprise at her dramatic abilities. In a review for the *New York Times*, Bosley Crowther opined that 'Jane Wyman assumes with quiet authority the difficult role of the loyal girl who loves and assists the central character and finally helps regenerate him' (1947: 2128). This success was to lead to more serious roles in films such as *The Yearling* (1946), *Johnny Belinda* (1948), *Stagefright* (1950), the first filmed version of *The Glass Menagerie* (1950) and *The Blue Veil* (1951). In this more 'serious' phase of her career, Wyman eschewed the glamour of musicals and comedy and gained recognition for her willingness to take on challenging roles; ageing from a young to an older woman (*The Blue Veil*) or playing an emotionally repressed and physically impaired character (*The Glass Menagerie* and *Johnny Belinda*). In preparation for the latter role, she famously learned sign language, refusing to speak in company, much to the frustration of her husband Ronald Reagan, and blocked her ears with wax on set. Such commitment to her craft resulted in an Oscar for Best Actress in 1948 (her second nomination) and she was to gain further accolades with another two

Jane Wyman with Hitchcock on the set of
Stage Fright (1950)

Academy Award nominations (one for *Magnificent Obsession*), four Golden Globes and two Emmies.

Jane Wyman is quickly introduced in *Magnificent Obsession* as a point of identification for the assumed majority female audience but also as an aspirational figure, with her modern, open-topped sports car, modish coiffure and immaculate up-to-the-minute costumes designed by Bill Thomas to imitate Christian Dior's 'New Look'.[10] The film is a luxurious spectacle featuring extensive location work, presenting a vision of affluent post-war American life, filmed in widescreen by Sirk's frequent collaborator, cinematographer Russell Metty, exploiting to the full the expressive possibilities of the Technicolor process.

Magnificent Obsession was, as we have already noted, a remake of John Stahl's 1935 film and it is instructive to observe the ways in which the production and, more importantly, the performances differ between the two releases. The movie tells the convoluted story of the redemption of Bob Merrick, a playboy whose carelessness accidentally results in the death of a philanthropic doctor and, through a further twist of fate, the blindness of his wife (Helen Hudson in the 1935 version and Helen Phillips in 1954). In time, Merrick falls in love with the widowed Helen and becomes her constant companion, while she is unaware of his true identity for the majority of the film as those around her surprisingly remain silent on the subject to protect her feelings. Ultimately, the guilt-wracked Merrick has to give up his old life, subscribe to the deceased doctor's philosophy (i.e., a belief in anonymous gestures of kindness) and, perhaps most improbably of all, learn to become a pioneering brain surgeon in order to redeem himself and to save not only Helen's sight but also her life.

The 1935 screen version of Lloyd C. Douglas's bestselling novel of 1929 was a huge commercial hit for Universal. Indeed, it was so successful that the two stars (Irene Dunne and Robert Taylor) reprised their roles in 1937 for a Lux Radio Theatre production.

Often popularly derided as soap opera, the film did indeed result in more than one especially popular 'soap opera'.[11] While Stahl's film profited by Irene Dunne's established stardom, it also transformed the younger actor Robert Taylor into one of Hollywood's most popular leading men.

There are some quite obvious differences in the treatment and characterisation of the protagonists between the two films. For example, in the earlier film, Irene Dunne projects an air of hauteur in both deportment and voice. She spoke (like so many actresses of her generation) with a rather stagey, Anglicised pronunciation and diction, using so-called American theatre standard English.[12] Her statuesque figure, emphasised by costume, bearing (she seems much taller than her reported 5' 5") and a 'ladylike' performance of old world gentility, situates her character as one of refinement and breeding. By contrast, Wyman's much more naturalistic performance style means that her Helen, though still privileged, seems to be a 'modern' woman who audiences might more easily identify with as well as aspire to be.

However, the most striking differences are between the depictions of the playboy Bob Merrick (Robert Merrick in the 1935 version) performed by Robert Taylor and Hudson. Taylor plays Merrick as a wisecracking seducer with a style of delivery that would be equally at home in the screwball comedies of the same period. Indeed, an element of comedy runs all the way through Stahl's film that (intentionally or otherwise) draws attention to the rather implausible storyline. Taylor's animated physicality, often jumping around or tensed and ready for action, lends his Merrick a mercurial quality markedly different to the empty playboy that Hudson plays for Sirk in 1954. While the intentions of the films are very similar, the outcomes differ markedly from beginning to end. Stahl's film, despite being clearly intended to provoke tears, has a lightness of tone quite unlike the much more lavishly mounted and yet definitively darker version produced by Sirk.

Robert Taylor's light-hearted performance in
the 1935 version of *Magnificent Obsession*

At a key stage in his career then, Hudson faced the challenge
of taking on a popular and recognisable role, one that demanded a
shift in performance tone and style as the narrative progresses.
Additionally, his director sought to make strategic use of his
physicality and representative quality, demanding a performance
style that both draws attention to the flaws and inconsistencies of the
story while doing so by playing the material 'straight'. As David Bret
recounts in his biography of the actor, Hudson rose to the challenge,
irrespective of Sirk's opinion of his range or intellect. Bret notes:

Rock's performance was singled out by Bosley Crowther, the infamously
acerbic film critic with the *New York Times*. Though he was not overly fond of

the production as a whole, he wrote of its star, 'The strapping, manly Rock Hudson gives a fine, direct account of himself – in the film's only real surprise.' (2005: 45)

Foster Hirsch, in an essay on Hudson and Doris Day in *Larger than Life: Movie Stars of the 1950s*, writes that 'in *Magnificent Obsession* Hudson and Wyman perform in a hushed style that attains a quasi-mystical aura' (2010: 160). This interpretation of the performance register of Sirk's film draws attention not only to the distanced liminal quality of Hudson's style, mirrored in Wyman's 'hushed', muted performance of grief and loss of hope, but also to the cool detachment of the director's approach. One of the most striking aspects of *Magnificent Obsession* is the extent to which Sirk simultaneously emotionally implicates the viewer in the drama and, at the same time, creates what has been regarded as an ironic distance from what has often been decried as tawdry source material. Charles Affron, for example, notes 'the comic-inspirational mode the director uses for the endings of *Magnificent Obsession* and *All That Heaven Allows*, with their heavily conclusive, posterish iconography (a painted backdrop of a desert, a deer grazing in the forest)' (1980: 51). The use of an ironic *mise en scène* (seen as the determining characteristic of Sirk's authorship) produces an artificiality in *Magnificent Obsession* and, as will be seen in its 'sequel', *All That Heaven Allows* (1955), that draws attention to the beautiful surfaces, consumerist ideals and social conservatism that the director regards as hollow.

Throughout the film, which is thematically concerned with vision in both a physical and metaphorical sense, Hudson is presented as a spectacle.[13] We are encouraged to admire his physical beauty and to simultaneously disapprove of his moral values. This, in itself, calls for a level of poise and restraint, as he is required to shift between arrogance and charm from scene to scene and sometimes within a single scene. From the opening sequence, in which his speedboat crashes after racing across and disrupting the peace of a placid lake (and the other characters around him), we are confronted with a character who is both reckless and self-obsessed. It is not until we see him confined to his hospital bed following his accident that his motivations and character are fully revealed to us. Unlike Taylor's carefree, light-hearted Merrick, Hudson's is an impatient and thoughtless rich boy, smoking cigarettes and making phone calls from his hospital bed. With a callous lack of sensitivity to those around him he attempts to assuage his guilt about the respirator that was used to resuscitate him at the expense of Dr Phillips's life, with money rather than a demonstration of any genuine remorse. In a bar scene following his exit from hospital, Hudson performs Merrick as a nihilistic playboy, convincingly drunk and rejecting the advances of a blonde. Once again here, rather than Robert Taylor's wisecracking devil-may-care Merrick, Hudson's character seems jaded and world-weary, a man for whom money has only brought empty hedonism. Subsequently, the feckless Merrick is not only the inadvertent cause of Dr Phillips's death but, following a rather misjudged attempt at seduction that ends with Helen stepping in front of a speeding car, he is equally responsible for her blindness. It is this event that initially results in a shift in performance from reckless nihilism to quiet remorse and dutiful incognito friendship. In a scene at the lake, the venue of the initial accident that set the drama in progress, the blind Helen passes the time with a young girl who acts as her eyes. As the camera follows the youngster walking towards the lake and describing the scene, Hudson's Merrick is revealed to the audience sitting behind the couple, silently smoking, his back turned as he witnesses what unfolds. This fragment is, in many ways, an illustration and prescient indicator of the liminal character of so many of the parts that Hudson played. He is an unseen observer although, as we discover, Helen is aware of his presence. Merrick hereafter assumes the identity of 'Robbie Robertson' in order to become Helen's companion, disguising himself and his guilt, until

Hudson and Wyman shooting *Magnificent Obsession* on location (1954)

eventually they fall in love. Helen travels to Europe in the hope that her sight can be restored and this leads to the first emotional crescendo of the film. Designed by Sirk with what can only be described as ruthless efficiency, eliciting the maximum emotional response at this point in the narrative, only the hardest heart would be unmoved by Wyman's realisation that her sight will not be restored. With a background track of plangent violins and dissonant bass chords struck out on a piano (Sirk's favourite device to signify a moment of tragedy), the music emphasises the pathos of the scene. Wyman's affecting performance and the reaction shots of a room of doctors in a sequence of close-ups are ironically situated in a brightly lit consulting room. The emotional stakes are raised further in the subsequent scene, by contrast now set in darkness, when Helen struggles to find her way in the unfamiliar lodgings. Here Helen's desolation reduces her companion Joyce (Barbara Rush) to tears when she tells her that 'Tomorrow there won't be a dawn for me.' She follows this line with 'Forgive me, Joyce, I didn't mean to parade my emotions.' This piece of dialogue reveals the key to the performance style of both this film and the one to follow. Emotions are not 'paraded' at all by any of the actors (least of all Hudson and Wyman) but rather kept very much in check. The emotional parade is provided instead by the *mise en scène*, lighting, camerawork and Frank Skinner's swooning orchestral score, in this case freely pastiching Beethoven and sometimes absurd in its high romantic intensity. Hudson arrives at the end of this scene and tries to lift Helen's spirits as he moves towards his final emotional transformation from guilt to purposefulness. The ensuing dimly lit scenes of European 'romance' are ironic in their evocations of chocolate-box clichés, underscoring the tragedy of the predicament, highlighting the fact that Helen is blind in a physical and also a symbolic sense to what is happening around her. It is while working in close proximity to another actor in these exchanges (usually in two shots and close-ups) that Hudson demonstrates his particular aptitude in romantic scenes. He speaks in soft, almost whispered tones, his deep voice suggesting an attentiveness to his partner that would no doubt live up to many of the female audience's dreams of a tall, dark and handsome man with eyes only for them. In these scenes, we see Hudson moving from a state of guilt, played out in quietness and acts of kindness, to a stoicism that marks his transformation (grey-haired by the end of the film) to a surgeon and man with a mission, now possessing the skills necessary to perform the improbable surgery that restores Helen's sight and rescues her life. With its complicated succession of coincidence and lags in narrative motivation, it is easy to deride *Magnificent Obsession* as trash (as has often happened). However, its emotional power is less easy to deny. The centrality of the performances of Hudson and Wyman to this emotional impact, both actors bringing a dignity to the film's rather more sensational aspects, accounts for its huge commercial and popular success and Hudson acquiring the new status of a major Hollywood star.[14]

All That Heaven Allows (Douglas Sirk, 1955)

All That Heaven Allows, made the following year and expressly designed to cash in on the box-office success of *Magnificent Obsession*, has become something of a touchstone text for subsequent film-makers, including Rainer Werner Fassbinder and Todd Haynes and, alongside *Written on the Wind*, is probably the film that most clearly epitomises what is now understood as the Sirkian style. An advertisement in *Life* magazine summarises the film's popular appeal:

This is the adult story of Cary Scott who wanted love but was afraid of it, afraid of her children's scorn and the names her friends would call her … afraid of her own surging passions … yet powerless to resist them!

This is the tender story of two people who wanted all of each other that Heaven would allow!

This is the great story that reunites those magnificent stars of *Magnificent Obsession*. (1955: 11)

Wyman is once again cast as a widow but this time the age difference between the two actors is emphasised, with the drama hinging on the 'sensational' prospect of an 'older' woman's romantic relationship with a younger man from a different social class.[15] Hudson is cast as Ron Kirby, the son of the previous (and now deceased) gardener, who falls in love with the lonely Cary Scott much to the outrage of her children and the rest of the wealthy bourgeois community of Stoningham. Whereas Bob Merrick in *Magnificent Obsession* is a feckless playboy who is redeemed through hard work and self-sacrifice and changed in the process, Ron is stoic, self-contained from the outset and devoid of any self-doubt. Consequently, *All That Heaven Allows* demands a different performance style of Hudson. He is required to act, drawing on the modality of one of the perennial masculine archetypes of American popular culture, 'the strong silent type' while simultaneously conveying an air of (albeit ill-defined) enigma. The story is in part about Cary's desire for the different type of life that Ron seems to represent and her efforts to understand his motivations and, subsequently, to rethink her own fears and prejudices.

From the opening scene in which Cary first encounters Ron, clearing her garden for the autumn, we understand that there is an attraction but also a rift (in values and expectations) between the couple. This is expressed through *mise en scène* (notably costume) and through performance. Ron initially runs to Cary's aid to carry a box of plates and is rewarded for his gallantry by an invitation to share lunch with her on the patio. In the scene, which establishes the nature of their relationship and what is to happen next, costume initially signifies difference. Hudson is dressed in workmen's clothing in neutral, khaki tones that appear appropriate to his profession, social role and his connection via horticulture to nature. Wyman, in a conservative grey tweed suit and pearls, coordinates with the elegant grey and white clapboarding of the family home and the suburban ideals of comfort and respectability that her environment suggests. This elaborately overdetermined *mise en scène*, characteristic of Sirk and put to particularly effective use here, creates a stifling atmosphere in which every gesture and object carries meaning and must in part account for the film's enduring fascination with cineastes and directors alike. Hudson's performance is once again muted, this time however signifying that Ron Kirby (who we discover later on lives by the principles of Thoreau's *Walden; or, Life in the Woods* [1854]) is a man of nature who has turned his back on polite society. While Wyman offers him sandwiches and coffee in a fussy and maternal manner (perhaps mirroring the conclusion of the film, where she will have to nurse the incapacitated Ron back to health), he only makes eye contact periodically, providing minimal verbal responses to her questions and only becoming animated (smiling and showing enthusiasm) when he is able to talk about plants and his plans to study at agricultural college. This performance of self-containment is structured as the trigger for Cary's initial interest in the younger man, which over time transforms into romance. Although the nature of their relationship changes over the course of the narative, Hudson maintains an air of gnomic enigma throughout, which means that Kirby seems by turns self-controlled and self-determined and, as Laura Mulvey has implied, a distant (and I would argue liminal) idealised figure (1987: 78–9). As Ron will not change his views, Cary will have to if she wants to share a life with him. Ron is an ideal but like all ideals he is both difficult to live up to and difficult to like.

Hudson here uses his voice, already deep in tone, to suggest introversion and distance through the slow, deliberate, pensive delivery of his lines. Even in the famously awkward scene in which, having been presented to Cary's friends at the country club, Ron physically threatens the local lothario Howard, his voice never rises above a quietly determined 'You'd better stay right where you are.' This is one of the rare moments to hint at an alternative, possibly repressed, aspect to Ron's personality.[16] In *All That Heaven Allows*, a film that has largely overshadowed *Magnificent Obsession* both in critical accounts and reputation, Hudson consolidates his position as the major new star of the era with a performance of masculinity that establishes the ideal male as a man of few words.

Acting and 'behaving'

By the middle of the 1950s, the performance register developed by Hudson became the hallmark of his acting style for the remainder of his career, providing a surprisingly flexible framework (as we shall see) for working in a range of genres and with a variety of actors and directors. This register manifests itself as a very particular, underplayed naturalism that is meant to convey self-containment, suggesting interiority through quietness rather than broad gesture. It is naturally important to remember that performance styles are both culturally specific and temporally grounded. So, just as nineteenth-century theatrical naturalism might appear extremely melodramatic to modern audiences, similarly, 1950s 'method' acting (the paradigm of dramatic 'authenticity'), can seem tricksy and affected in retrospect. Likewise, as I will reiterate in the final chapter, Hudson's solemnity in both *Magnificent Obsession* and *All That Heaven Allows* can tend to be read, through a satirising gaze, as so overdetermined as to be comedic. Although this would be to misunderstand the intentions of these performances and a dismissive appraisal of this kind of acting and its purveyors, it's notable that even contemporaneous accounts of film acting (in particular the work of Hollywood stars like Hudson) tend to draw attention to the perceived flaws of many screen actors.

Cynthia Baron has noted that by the 1930s and 40s drama teachers were producing acting manuals for those working (or aspiring to work) in American cinema (2004: 83–93). During the same period and onwards, a vigorous debate emerged among critics, actors and scholars about the nature and particularities of screen acting and the differences between acting for the stage and the screen. The positions that the various interested parties take in these debates are often polarised (this remains a characteristic of much debate around screen acting) and usually concerned with distinguishing between the qualities of a good actor and the characteristics of 'bad' acting. Good acting is in almost every case identified as emerging from a training on the stage and an immersion in the discipline of what I will describe for simplicity's sake here as 'classical acting'. Acting then is professionalised and becomes a skill developed through formal training. Bad acting, on the other hand, is ostensibly regarded as demonstrating a lack of expertise or technical virtuosity. Inevitably, therefore, given the technical specifics of cinema as a medium (described in Pudovkin's seminal *Film Technique and Film Acting* [1953]) the naturalistic, underplayed acting often called for in cinema has seemed to many critics to demonstrate many of the indices of bad acting.

Film stars, in particular, tended to be singled out for quite scathing critique. For example, in his 1953 essay 'Stereotypes, and Acting in Films', Arthur Knight (author of *The Liveliest Art*, published in 1957), demonstrates the degree to which the work of film actors was often considered disparagingly:

The stars, as professional types, are similarly incorporated by the skilled director into his narrative. They 'become plastic material' which he can shape and mould at his discretion. Considering the basic ability of many a star performer, this is an especially sound procedure. (1953: 5)

In a similar vein, the character actor Alexander Knox, in a 1946 essay entitled 'Acting and Behaving', makes a distinction between those professionals who are trained and skilled actors and those who he sees as merely 'behaving':

Behaving is a form of acting which can be used to display the same kind of empty idealizations that fill some of the popular magazines and pass for human beings. ... Behaving is the form of acting without which second-rate dramatists would be completely lost. ... Acting seems to me to be behaving plus interpretation. (1946: 263)

The performance style that Hudson had begun to master by the mid-1950s would presumably have been regarded by Knox, Knight and others as the epitome of 'behaving' rather than acting. Indeed, this attitude towards this type of screen acting has found its way into (and now pervades) both the scholarship and the popular accounts assessing Hudson. So it has been tempting for many commentators to take Sirk's lead in describing Hudson's 'simplicity' and 'fixity' as if these seemingly innate qualities were mere behaviours captured by the skilled director rather than being 'performed' on screen, assuming therefore that they did not require acting skills. In this formulation, the on-screen ease that marks Hudson out is the very thing that is dismissed as not 'acting' at all. My contention, however, is that the contrary is true, that Hudson's 'solidity' is the result of the craft of a team of professionals (including Sirk) and that at the heart of that activity is the actor himself. At the zenith of his stardom in the 1950s, Hudson represented ideals of masculinity that were, in his particular case, both about 'acting' on screen and 'behaving' on and off screen like the ideal modern man. In short, the argument that Richard Maltby makes in *Hollywood Cinema* (2003) that the screen actor has two bodies (the body of the actor and the body of the character) fold in on each other in Hudson's case.

It is productive here to compare Hudson's performed model of masculinity with some of his contemporaries. While we could draw comparisons with any number of actors (for example, Kirk Douglas, Burt Lancaster, William Holden and even the young Clint Eastwood), an especially useful point of comparison is offered by Charlton Heston, another figure associated with paradigmatic masculinity and famously described by Michel Mourlet as 'an axiom' of cinema (1991: 234).[17] Heston coincidentally went to the same school as Hudson in Winnetka but, unlike Hudson, worked as an actor on the stage and television prior to his move into cinema. Although Heston gained an Academy Award for *Ben Hur* (1959), popular attitudes towards his acting remained ambivalent. While this is comparable to Hudson's critical reception in many respects, the difference in Heston's case is that as an actor he most definitely *is* acting whenever he is on screen. Famous for taking roles in historical and biblical epics, his performance style works best when it is matched to material on an epic scale. His stentorian, declamatory tones and often mannered performances produce a sense of a stridently heroic masculinity. By contrast, Hudson's muted dramatic palette is perhaps more emotionally legible to modern audiences and works especially well when set up as a foil in contrast to more vertiginous, stylised displays of dramatic technique.

Written on the Wind (Douglas Sirk, 1956)

Perhaps the best example of Hudson's muted performance of masculinity deployed as a counterpoint to a more stylised and exaggerated acting style can be found in *Written on the Wind*. The auteurist account of Sirk's career has it that there is a division in the films of the Universal period between projects that the director worked on out of necessity (usually with Ross Hunter as producer) and those that were more 'personal' and made with greater autonomy (often in collaboration with Albert Zugsmith). As Jon Halliday comments, 'In *Imitation of Life*, Sirk is fighting – and transcending – the universe of Fannie Hurst and Ross Hunter … . In *Written on the Wind*, he is able to express more directly his vision of America' (1972: 8).

Adapted from Robert Wilder's 1945 novel of the same name (reputedly based on real events) the book's adult subject matter was given a racy cinematic treatment, as it recounts the unhappy story of Marylee and Kyle Hadley, heirs to the Hadley oil empire, for whom wealth and privilege have brought nothing but unhappiness. Marylee (Dorothy Malone) is a 'shameless' nymphomaniac (a sensationally lurid character trait for mid-1950s Hollywood) who has never been able to reconcile her unrequited love for childhood friend and working-class boy Mitch (Hudson.) Kyle (Robert Stack) is by contrast an impotent alcoholic playboy (by turns sensational and contradictory) who is riddled with jealousy towards his friend Mitch and the closeness that develops between Mitch and Kyle's wife Lucy (Lauren Bacall). Regardless of the persuasiveness of the claims that Sirk's best work emerged when he was freed from the controlling hands of Ross Hunter (*Written on the Wind* is no less of a populist 'potboiler' than the Hunter/Sirk films and lacks the tearjerking emotional punch of the Hunter collaborations), it is notable that Sirk cast Hudson as his leading man in the two films often cited as the examples of this 'purer' cinematic output: *Written on the Wind* and *The Tarnished Angels*. The difference here is that, whereas in the films that established both his and Hudson's success, the actor was positioned as an archetype of romantic ideals of manhood, in both of these later films he is more akin to the everyman or narrator/observer. In both cases, he is positioned in one way or another as an outsider and the liminality of this status is perhaps even more marked in these films than in either *Magnificent Obsession* or *All That Heaven Allows*.

Written on the Wind is a particularly revealing case study, highlighting how Hudson's acting style is productively played off against the more histrionic dramatic registers of Dorothy Malone and Robert Stack. At a straightforward level, the film could easily serve to reinforce the validity of Arthur Knight's opinions on the limited ability of most star players (in this case, Hudson and Lauren Bacall), who need to be supported by a skilled director when pitted against actors who have 'craft', such as Stack and Malone. Similarly, the film could also illustrate Knox's comments, identifying Malone and Stack's 'acting' in opposition to Hudson and Bacall's 'behaving'. However, such arguments tend to devalue the strategic casting in operation here and, instead, reproduce commonsense understandings of acting as conspicuous displays of technique. Rather, I would argue that what can be seen in Hudson's work in these films is an increasingly nuanced and subtle screen acting style that complements and counterpoints the excesses of the supporting actors and the elaborate *mise en scène*. In *Written on the Wind*, Hudson's (and Bacall's) naturalism, belonging to the representational acting tradition, is deliberately engaged in conjunction with Stack and Malone's much more stylised and excessive performances that enlist a semaphore acting method of poses and movements to convey emotional states that in execution approaches Delsartian gesturalism.[18] Critical accounts of Sirk's work during his 1970s 'rediscovery' often connected his film-making practices with the theatre of Brecht.[19] The mannered, expressive movements of both Stack and Malone provide some evidence of this and can seem to employ a Brechtian degree of presentational stylisation during moments of high drama in the film.

Written on the Wind has a dramatic tempo and sense of urgency that are completely unlike anything in the previous two Sirk films discussed in this chapter. Within the opening few minutes, we witness Kyle's death, motivating a flashback to the months prior to this incident. Here, Mitch and Lucy are introduced in a scene in a glamorous Manhattan design office (in which it is swiftly revealed that Lucy is 'only a secretary'). Not only does this establish these two characters as the film's main protagonists but also that there is a chemistry between them, indicated initially through Hudson's character slyly admiring Bacall's legs even before he has met her and later on confirmed by their flirtatious conversation and exchange of admiring glances. These short sequences quickly set up the characters of Mitch (as grounded, sensible, modest but resolutely 'manly') and Lucy (as a slightly cynical, sophisticated career woman, the type that Bacall was often associated with at this point in her career). The scene is then set for the two to meet up with Kyle at the equally modish venue of the '21' Club. Here, Kyle is revealed carousing with two women as Mitch enters the club with Lucy. Extravagantly stubbing out his cigarette in a full Martini glass, Kyle snubs his female companions to approach the couple, before swiftly extricating Lucy from Mitch. It is implied that this is a standard pattern of behaviour as well as an unwelcome one. While Stack's character introduces himself to Lucy, Hudson's face registers disapproval. Hudson's reaction here, as he reflects on the behaviour of characters around him, becomes a recurrent feature of his performance throughout the rest of this scene and the film as a whole. Stack's voice is remarkable from the outset, especially here: deep and mannered, his lines delivered as if he is reading advertising copy about himself. Kyle talks about himself in the third person, as if detached from himself, so it is 'Kyle Hadley' that leans in towards Bacall, putting his arm behind her while plying her with champagne. A reaction shot of Hudson places him at an observant distance from this hackneyed seduction scene, while his sardonic responses imply that he is accustomed to this type of behaviour and is familiar with being cast in the role of witness. Stack's glaring intensity and declamatory but rather robotic performance of romantic play is designed to be uncomfortable (and even rather offensive for a contemporary viewer) in comparison to the less forced interactions between Hudson and Bacall. In this scene Hudson's amused but disapproving assessment of the situation initially positions him as the audience's point of identification.

Hudson's role as the everyman 'observer' is emphasised once again in a scene at a local bar, close to the Hadley estate where Marylee is once again drunk (we presume this is a common occurrence) and in the arms of an unsuitable admirer. The scene is extraordinarily heightened and blocked in many respects like a scene from a theatrical production. Each of the key characters occupies a demarcated space on the screen, producing a series of tableaux, another device borrowed from Delsarte and theatrical melodrama. Stack (a short man) plays Kyle as self-important and ineffectual, while Malone's performance of drunkenness provides a dramatic motivation for the extremes of her movements and gestures: her pouting, crawling over furniture and rolling of her head in a sequence of hysterically feline movements. Initially, Hudson is pushed to the perimeter of these compositions but also to the foreground relative to the audience so that his attentiveness can be observed, along with the resigned familiarity on his face. He sits at the bar until called on to fight and restore order, after Kyle demonstrates his inability in combat and, therefore, his inadequacy as a man. However, one of the best examples of Hudson's subtle, nuanced acting comes during the following scene in Marylee's car. Here, Marylee reminisces and fantasises about their past, confessing the depth of her feelings (i.e., her desire) for Mitch and her hatred for Kyle, feelings that manifest themselves through her various extremes of behaviour. Hudson's reactions of disapproval, anger and disgust are played out almost in silence, largely through a clenched jaw and a shift between flashes of emotion and an impassive expression. As Lawrence Schaffer notes,

The faces of certain actors; Brando, Gielgud, Clift, March, Tracy, Bogart, seem to be acutely inner-reflective. These actors seem to be doing a good deal of thinking. Their faces look preoccupied, as if attending to some inner voice, or memory. The face, when not self-manipulated, shows what it does not know of itself. (1978: 6)

While Hudson might not automatically be thought of in the same company as Brando or Gielgud, his role in *Written on the Wind* demanded he demonstrate a refined technique, involving an economy of gesture and movement to express an interiority that was rarely, if ever, associated with him.

Hudson's minimalism is pitted even more fully against Malone and Stack's full armoury of Delsartian mannerism during the climactic scene of the film that leads to the dramatic moment shown during the opening sequence. Kyle (who by now suspects that Mitch is not only having an affair with his wife Lucy but is also the father of their child) returns from the bar, drunk and in a state of anguished jealousy. This is a moment of high drama in a film in which the dramatic stakes are already stratospheric, and Stack's performance

Mitch (Hudson) at the periphery of the drama
in *Written on the Wind* (1956)

here is perhaps at its most extreme. His voice is distorted by alcohol, sounding as though it is being pulled up from deep inside him, suggestive of deep-seated psychological pain. With eyes popping and body sweating and bleeding, he brandishes a gun at Mitch. His dramatic language is redolent of the gangster film. Here, Hudson's stature makes the more diminutive Stack seem pathetic rather than threatening. In short, he is a man at the end of the line, pushed into a corner and this final gesture is simultaneously futile and self-defeating. This heightened performance register is set against Hudson's who, after rushing into the library to confront Kyle, assumes a calm demeanour. He enters the library with his hands in his pockets, his face showing the caution that he otherwise masks. In contrast to Kyle's hysteria, his voice is low-pitched, revealing little emotion. Whereas Kyle's movements and gestures are erratic, Mitch is able to reason calmly. Meanwhile, Marylee enters the scene to raise the stakes further still. She runs down the sweeping staircase while leaves blow in through the open front door, her arms raised and then gracefully trailing behind her as she reaches the door of the library. Her expressive gestures evoke the self-dramatising heroine of Victorian melodrama. The drama of the scene in the library is amplified by Marylee's movements and, as Kyle becomes progressively irrational, the conflict between him and Mitch escalates. Delsarte's principles have at least in part informed this highly stylised sequence of physical contortions, facial reaction shots and 'melodramatic' gestures. Playing against Hudson's Mitch, who retains his status as the voice of reason, the stylisation and 'overacting' that both Malone and Stack deliberately deploy become yet more heightened. Mitch here is a witness to the emotional decay that wealth and privilege brings. Within the moral framework of the film, the naturalistic, downplayed masculinity that Hudson gives to Mitch stands as the measurement against which the Hadley children fail (i.e., Kyle's inadequate and impotent masculinity and Marylee's decadent and improper femininity). He is, as Barbara Klinger observes, 'an ideological anchor of sanity' (1994: 109). So, at the same time as being nominally positioned as the audience's point of identification, he is also an archetype, a model of idealised masculinity, one that is not only unattainable by Kyle Hadley but by the vast majority of the film's audience. As Hudson himself was to ironically note of the role, 'I am so pure I am impossible' (Oppenheimer and Vitek 1986: 59).

Hollywood style vs the 'method'

Just as Hudson's masculine performance was pitted against displays of neurosis and instability in *Written on the Wind*, he was often held up in contemporaneous media coverage as an exemplar of a modern masculinity, both as an actor and a personality, who was quintessentially suburban and domesticated. Just as frequently, this was presented as the antidote to the 'alternative' masculinities

Hudson's solidity pitted against the theatrics of
Dorothy Malone and Robert Stack in *Written
on the Wind* (1956)

epitomised by figures such as Marlon Brando and, more latterly, by
James Dean, two actors known for reckless and unruly behaviour.
As Barbara Klinger observes in a chapter on Hudson's star
signification in *Melodrama and Meaning* in fan magazines and
other popular publications, he was often associated with a life of
suburban affluence, recreation and consumerism. This inevitably
made him a popular figure with advertisers and a spokesperson
for a range of products as will be seen in the next chapter. By
contrast, Brando's press coverage focused on his hell-raising and
promiscuous private life, while much of Dean's publicity centred on
his idiosyncratic personal habits. Frequently, Hudson is cited as a
model of normality and furthermore one that stands in opposition

to the more challenging model of masculinity offered by Brando and Dean.

This confrontation between the 'clean-cut' masculinity of Hudson and the 'neurotic' masculinity of Brando and Dean (*et al.*) is perhaps most vividly dramatised (metaphorically and literally) in the clash of both personalities and performance style in evidence in the production of George Stevens's *Giant*, where Hudson was cast alongside James Dean. Accounts often suggest an antipathy between the two actors, one that extended beyond the personal and into the professional. Dean's method-influenced approach, insisting on immersion in a character, meant that he could be disruptive on set, difficult to direct and rude to his fellow actors (ibid.: 54).[20] For example, Dean reportedly told gossip columnist Hedda Hopper that Hudson was 'big and lumpy', declaring that he acted like 'a piece of wood'.[21] Hudson, by contrast, adhered to the established values of Hollywood professionalism, which included maintaining a scrupulous silence on matters relating to the conduct of his fellow actors. These differences in style and demeanour inevitably resulted in something of an off- and on-set clash between an established (and, for some, clichéd and moribund) Hollywood acting style and a 'new' and dynamic (but also unpredictable) method technique, as epitomised by Dean.

It is important to note that this clash was rather more to do with personality than it was to do with acting *per se* as both Hudson and Dean's performances are pitched in a register that must broadly be understood as naturalistic. The mechanisms through which that naturalism is achieved and how it manifests itself in the context of an actor's performance are the key differences here. So, although a dichotomy has often been set up between the proponents of the method and classical acting styles, this is largely a binarism that has been used to establish the credentials and reputations of figures like Marlon Brando, Montgomery Clift and James Dean rather than one that describes a fundamental difference in objective.[22] Nonetheless, contemporaneous debates around notions of masculinity and appropriate, socially sanctioned masculine conduct are dramatised and enacted in *Giant* through this 'difference' of acting styles.

Giant (George Stevens, 1956)

Adapted from Edna Ferber's 1952 novel, *Giant* is a Texan family saga, with an epic twenty-five-year scope, which had been serialised to great success in *Ladies Home Journal*. It was the largest production that Hudson was involved in, making significant demands on him as an actor and resulting in his only Oscar nomination. The role of Bick Benedict was challenging, requiring him to age from a young to a middle-aged man during the course of a film that is over three hours long. Once again, Hudson was cast as a man who becomes changed with time and experience. He begins the film as an old world Texan patriarch and bigot but is gradually transformed into a liberal, 'modern' man by the end.

The film's production history was both protracted and not without controversy. From the moment that she heard about plans for the production, Ferber was in regular contact with Stevens and became the film's co-producer. From the outset, she expressed her hopes that her intention for the book (an exploration of racial prejudice against Mexicans) would be respected. She was to become a fairly consistent critic of the way in which the production was developed, and even volunteered to work on a rewrite of the script. Unhappy with the changes that Stevens made to the story and with his casting choices, she felt that her voice was largely ignored. She was especially unhappy with the way in which the focus of the narrative was shifted away from the female lead to a focus on the destructive dynamics between Bick and Jett (James Dean). As Marilyn Moss notes, 'While recognizing Stevens's gifts as a director … Ferber argued, I feel that Leslie has to quite a degree, faded into a

Hudson and Taylor with George Stevens,
a director with a special talent for extracting
strong performances from his actors

somewhat pale character as the two leading male characters have taken on additional stature' (2004: 203–4).

Ferber's concerns here are only partly justified. While the film opens with Bick arriving in Maryland to buy a horse and (by inference) to acquire a wife, and it is true that the conflict between Bick and Jett dominates, the audience's sympathies, from the outset, are with Leslie (Elizabeth Taylor) and it is her journey to a new life, alongside her attempts to change the culture around her, that progress the narrative. Hudson's Bick is an archetypical Texan, a distant, unknowable figure once again. For his part, Stevens thought Ferber's characters were thin, underdeveloped clichés and he had worked with the scriptwriters to develop clearer motivations for their actions.

Ferber, as noted above, was reputedly also unhappy with the choice of lead actors. Bick Benedict was a major part and consequently a range of leading men were considered for the role. Ferber had wanted Burt Lancaster, while Clark Gable had also been mooted (ibid.: 214). Hudson was Stevens's selection, based on the strength of his performance in *Magnificent Obsession*. The director's commitment to his casting choice was demonstrated by commissioning Universal's acting coach, Estelle Harman, to help Hudson develop the character. Perhaps more surprisingly still, given the iconic status of her performance, Elizabeth Taylor was far from Stevens's first choice. A long list of actresses had been considered, with Audrey Hepburn the favoured option, and it was only when the services of Grace Kelly could not be secured that Taylor was cast.

In one of the many favourable reviews in the *Saturday Post* on the film's release in 1956, Hollis Alpert noted that 'Stevens is known for his ability to get hitherto unsuspected talents out of his actors' (1956: 28). While Alpert suggested that a large part of the interest in the film would be generated by James Dean's final screen performance (since he had died in a tragic car accident before filming was completed), he also commented that both Taylor and

Hudson acquitted themselves well. Undoubtedly a major reason for Stevens's success in extracting strong performances from actors were the specifics of his working practices. His approach to film-making made for slow progress, since it involved multiple takes of every shot from a variety of angles, with a performance subsequently put together in the edit suite during post-production. While this resulted in the 'best' takes being used to construct a well-rounded set of screen performances, the technique also entailed lengthy shooting schedules and meant that *Giant* significantly exceeded its original budget. Taylor's lengthy bouts of ill health, as well as Dean's death, meant that the film's epic scale was matched by a similarly momentous production schedule.

While the film made significant demands on the whole cast, this was especially the case for the leads, Hudson and Taylor, who were required to convey a lifetime of emotional ups and downs, including births, marriages and deaths. Interestingly however, the scenes that best demonstrate Hudson's emerging confidence and accomplishments as an actor are in fact those in which he is paired with Dean. These scenes also illustrate how Stevens 'created' an actor's performance through framing, editing and controlling physical parameters. For example, the first scene to establish the peculiar dynamics of the relationship between Bick Benedict and Jett Rink takes place when the newlyweds Bick and Leslie arrive at the Benedicts' family home, the remote and bleak Reata. Having briefly introduced his wife to the household, Bick quickly rushes out to confront Jett, who is driving his car without permission. The confrontation takes place on the veranda, as will so many of the pivotal moments of the first part of the film.

During this sequence, the screen door acts as a proscenium arch, narrowing the audience's field of vision and framing the actors in order to draw attention to the conflict in this relationship by conveying it physically and dramatically by the use of space. When Hudson steps out onto the porch, through a screen door, the frame

A carefully constructed *mise en scène* illustrates the emotional drama between Bick (Hudson) and Jett (James Dean) in *Giant* (1956)

is shrunk by the use of blank space and light shining through the door frame, narrowing the world of the story to the confines of the conflict between the two men. Placed in the foreground, Hudson's physicality (his sheer bulk) is highlighted so that he seems to fill at least a third of the screen space. Meanwhile, his stillness and centredness position him as calm but also a potentially threatening patriarch. In contrast, Dean is placed in the middle distance (initially seated in the car but then standing beside it) away from Bick, while Leslie and Bick's sister Luz (Mercedes McCambridge) occupy the lower part of the frame. Shot from this high angle, Dean seems smaller than he already is. He also noticeably twitches with nervous energy, while Hudson hardly moves throughout this sequence other than to turn his head at key moments, revealing his profile. His restraint signifies an anger that is contained and controlled. Moreover, Hudson seems lit up as he is filmed through the screen door, with this soft-focus treatment serving to make him appear something of an idealised figure, heroically asserting his authority and all the more impenetrable as a character due to his positioning within the *mise en scène*. The scene culminates in Jett's skulking retreat. In an exceptionally effective piece of physical theatre, Dean deliberately falls back off the porch in a curiously sinister fashion, as if he is being sucked back down into the earth. Overall, the scene demonstrates the asymmetry of the power dynamics of their relationship (which will be challenged later on in the film) through a combination of framing, editing and performance.

The final scene of the first half of the film sets up Jett's change of fortune when he strikes oil on land given to him as part of the settlement of Luz's will. Dean's character drives his dilapidated truck erratically towards Reata, the gradual progress of his approach and arrival across the barren territory viewed from the far distance, indicating not just the vastness of the Texan landscape but also the huge rift between Jett and Bick that is about to be abruptly confronted. The Benedicts, along with their friends and family, are seated on the porch of Reata in their finery, all uniformly dressed in light neutral tones. Hudson and Taylor, in particular, are immaculately groomed for this key scene. In contrast, Dean is covered from head to foot in oil and hysterical at the prospect of his newfound wealth. As in the earlier scene, the staging renders this moment particularly theatrical. Hudson and Taylor, dignified and never more physically beautiful than they were at this precise instant, maintain a cool composure at a moment when their position within this largely agrarian community is under threat from the destructive forces of a 'new' technology and a new undignified and uncivilised Texas, represented by Dean's character. As Jett's diatribe becomes more menacing, he climbs the steps of the porch, threatening the domestic idyll, with the camera tilting up to give the impression that he is physically growing in stature. Hudson, leaning in a statuesque fashion against the pillar of the porch, regards him impassively until

Jett places his foot onto the porch. At this moment, there is a cut to a point-of-view midshot of the couple that pans between Dean and Hudson and Dean and Taylor. The scene culminates in a scuffle in which Jett appears to have won (for the time being at least). In the process, Bick's immaculate Sunday best clothes are stained literally and metaphorically by Jett's oily hands.

It has been noted elsewhere that Hudson and Taylor's performances have stood the test of time better than that of James Dean. Richard Dyer, for instance, has written that,

Dean's Method style now looks mannered: arched torso, hunched shoulders, shifting eyes, staccato speech ... . By comparison Rock is still, straight, unfussy, just there in the classic manner of Hollywood stars. Dean's style connotes naturalism, an acting convention associated in the period with awkwardness and neurotic emotionality. Rock's style suggests a different sense of the natural, namely normality. (2001: 162)

However, the 'normality' that Hudson's performances represent in this and other films of the period, is far from simple or uniform, as I have tried to illustrate throughout this chapter. In *Giant*, it is a normality that initially upholds traditional conservative values (including racist attitudes) that over time becomes the 'normality' of liberal contemporary values. In effect, Hudson's underplayed performances demonstrate the contingency and fluidity of normativity.

The military hero

Though Hudson is typically associated with romantic leads, during the mid- to late 1950s, he was also frequently cast in roles that exemplify the second of Paula Black's models of modern masculinity, the military hero (2004: 36–7). Inevitably with an actor as prolific as

Hudson (with over seventy-five screen credits to his name), areas of his career fall outside the scope of a study of this kind. As mentioned in the first chapter, Hudson's early successes emerged from small parts in Westerns, for example, and he continued to be sporadically involved with this genre throughout his career, notably alongside Dorothy Malone and Kirk Douglas in *The Last Sunset* (1961) and John Wayne in *The Undefeated* (1969). His masculine star persona also meant that he was cast in dramas such as *Twilight for the Gods* (1959), in a role one could easily imagine Humphrey Bogart playing, and *Something of Value* (1957), set within the contemporary context of Kenya's Mau Mau uprising. However, it was the role of the military professional that recurred consistently throughout his career, from an inauspicious screen debut in the war film *Fighter Squadron* (1948) to *Ice Station Zebra* (1968).

Although Hudson had been cast in a military role in *Air Cadet* in 1951, it was not until he gained star status that he was to return to playing the military man. By this time, the propagandist celebrations of military life and the wartime heroes of post-World War II Hollywood such as *Fighter Squadron* and *Air Cadet* had given way to films that were much more focused on the aftermath of conflict and concomitant crises. As Mike Chopra Grant notes,

The place of the ex-serviceman in post-war society was one of the major issues of the period immediately following the end of the war. ... concerns centred on the effects that the combination of training in the efficient use of violence and the brutalizing experiences of military service may have had on the psychological disposition of returning veterans, and consequently on their behaviour on returning to civilian life. (2006: 95)

These issues resulted in films explicitly about coming to terms with the trauma of war, played out in dramas of loss, regret, reconciliation and occasional redemption. So, for example, in *Never Say Goodbye* (1956) Hudson is a surgeon who encounters a wife he had thought dead and, through an extensive use of flashback, the story deals with his emotional trauma and fear that his own actions had caused their estrangement.[23] In *Battle Hymn* (1957), based on a true (if disputed) story, Hudson plays Dean Hess, a bomber pilot who became a minister following the war. Wracked with feelings of guilt that his actions resulted in the destruction of a German orphanage, he returns to the military in Korea to set up an orphanage for local children to atone for his deeds. Perhaps most notably, Hudson was cast as Frederick Henry opposite Jennifer Jones as Catherine Barkley in a lavish remake of *A Farewell to Arms* (1957). Ernest Hemingway's story of a wounded ambulance driver who falls in love with a nurse is a famously bleak indictment of the horrors of war, so bleak in fact that in the first screen adaptation in 1932 (directed by Frank Borzage and starring Gary Cooper and Helen Hayes), the story was altered to have a happy ending. Charles Vidor's 1957 version, which remained true to the original story by retaining an ending that speaks emphatically of loss, failed to please either Hemingway or the critics. Hemingway was especially unhappy that Jones, then thirty-eight, was playing a younger woman and it was this specific casting that tended to inform critical responses. Although also subject to criticism for his performance, Hudson was spared the majority of the invective heaped on Jones. Hollis Alpert's review is typical: 'Rock Hudson, of the mild manner and the pleasant, but vaguely confused face, is better. He is plausibly a young man caught between idealism and the horrifying confusions of war' (1958: 27).

It is apparent that, on the whole, in these military films Hudson utilised many of the same performance methods as in his romantic roles, with only occasional variances in terms of register or range. This is partly accounted for by the fact that such films tend to use the circumstances of war as a backdrop either for a romantic drama or the enactment of the reformation of a character and, as such, tend to map directly onto Hudson's romantic roles (especially those discussed earlier in this chapter). It is also no doubt due to the fact that in several of his military and romantic movies Hudson worked with the same directors (most notably Douglas Sirk).

There was, however, another category of military films in which Hudson tended to star, particularly during the 1960s. These deal with the lives of military career men, exploring the professionalised nature of combat and military life. Here Hudson is typically required to summon up a professionalised, managerial mode of bearing and conduct to play a figure of authority and maturity. For example, in Delbert Mann's *A Gathering of Eagles* (1963), Hudson is a B-52 commander charged with bringing high professional standards to his team during the years of the Cold War. Interestingly, Mann had already directed Hudson alongside Doris Day in the comedy *Lover Come Back* (1961). Rod Taylor was also in *A Gathering of Eagles*, an Australian who, having established himself as a popular TV actor, had played a minor role in *Giant* in 1956, graduating to lead in *The Time Machine* (1960) and *The Birds* (1961). In *A Gathering of Eagles*, it is obvious that Taylor was being positioned as a new heartthrob, very much in the mould of Hudson. It is perhaps no surprise then that he was to subsequently replace Hudson as Doris Day's partner in the later sex comedies *Do Not Disturb* (1965) and *The Glass Bottomed Boat* (1966). While the promotional material for *A Gathering of Eagles* clearly establishes Hudson as the film's star, it is also apparent that Taylor was being built up as the nascent star and the next best thing. Accordingly, both actors are presented as exemplars of a managerial professionalism that, as will be seen in the next chapter, was to become one of the key discourses of American masculinity as the 1950s gave way to the 60s. While indicating that a new generation of Hollywood male stars were lining up to replace Hudson at this time, *A Gathering of Eagles* also pointed towards the direction that Hudson's casting in military-themed films would take. So, for instance, in *Tobruk* (1967), Hudson was an expert topographer leading a team of commandos on an attack on a fuel-storage facility in the Sahara Desert. Meanwhile, in *Ice Station Zebra*

Hudson in *Ice Station Zebra* (1968)

in 1968, he played another authority figure, this time captain of a US military submarine who must transport troops to the North Pole.

By the late 1960s, John Sturges had demonstrated a particular talent for working with large (often star-studded) all-male ensemble casts, securing major commercial successes with films such as *The Magnificent Seven* (1960) and *The Great Escape* (1963). Here, he was able to capitalise on the diversity of acting styles and methods that his casts could bring to bear on a production. For example, he made full use of Yul Brynner's idiosyncratic mannerist performances, Steve McQueen's status as an emerging star and Eli Wallach's method acting in *The Magnificent Seven*. Similarly, in *The Great Escape*, he not only exploited dynamic American performance styles (e.g., those of McQueen, James Coburn and Charles Bronson) but combined these with the markedly different and rather more theatrical English performances of Donald Pleasence, Richard Attenborough and David McCallum. Sturges's *Ice Station Zebra* has an equally strong and diverse cast, one that enabled the director to play one performance style off against another. This is particularly noticeable in the scenes in which Hudson works alongside Patrick McGoohan. Like Hudson, McGoohan's performance style is one that is marked by a certain still, self-possessed quality. However, McGoohan's stillness often seems to suggest a contained threat or menace, an anger or aggression that might emerge in an outburst of unexpected violence. This is quite unlike the stoic self-assuredness implied by Hudson's quietude. The contrast is particularly evident in an early scene where Hudson's Commander Ferraday tries to uncover the nature of David Jones's (McGoohan) mission. While Jones settles into his cabin, Ferraday questions him in what appears to be a casual manner. Hudson plays Ferraday as a disinterested but knowing partner in this exchange of words, casually seated and removing a letter from his jacket while coolly appraising Jones. McGoohan engages the device of taking off his coat and hat while opening an attaché case to convey a mixture of mystery and threat that manifests itself in the most minute of gestures and modulations of vocal tone. While one actor (Hudson) uses a restrained style to indicate confidence and control, the other actor (McGoohan) uses an equally restrained register to indicate evasiveness, evoking an unsettling sense of himself as an enigma.

So, during the late 1950s and into the 60s, it is possible to observe a shift occurring in Hudson's career, from being cast as the romantic lead to playing mature authority figures. This transition, furthermore, indicates one of the directions that his career (like those of many of his contemporaries) would take, as he evolved from a leading screen heartthrob to a 'mature' actor. It is, moreover, this transition that will be the main focus of the final chapter.

3 'ADULT' CONTENT AND THE MATURE ACTOR

As the 1950s drew to a close, Rock Hudson was by all accounts one of the most successful and bankable stars in Hollywood. In little more than ten years, he had made the transition from an awkward bit part player to the major star of some of the biggest commercial and popular cinematic releases of the decade. This, now familiar, summary of Hudson's life, is one of a chance discovery and meteoric rise to fame and wealth. For example, in December 1958, *Life* magazine described Hudson as the 'modest ex-truck driver' who is now 'the biggest single box office draw in the US' (1958: 160).[1] This was in a round-up of Hollywood luminaries entitled 'People at the Top of Entertainment's World' with Hudson featured under the heading 'Box Office Champion'. The hyperbolic nature of stories of this kind notwithstanding, they tend to overlook, as revealed in the previous two chapters, the work that a team of interested parties had put into the construction of the actor's performances and his star image. Far from a stratospheric ascent to stardom, a consistent, collective effort had been the key to Rock Hudson's ultimate star status. The 1950s then was the most prolific period of Hudson's life as a film actor, a decade in which he appeared in thirty-eight films, which cemented his profile and success, while positioning him for the next major stage in his career. This next phase necessitated a further refinement in Hudson's image and dramatic repertoire, particularly as he shifted genres from romantic drama to adult comedy. This transition would also ensure that Hudson could maintain his career, unlike many of his contemporaries, by working in television. In many respects, Hudson's career path offers a case study for a mature actor during this time, as he moved from roles in which his youthful physicality and good looks were central to ones in which maturity, combined with a certain urbanity, were more important.

While the previous chapters have concerned a quite narrow timeframe, this final chapter has a much broader sweep, covering the period from the end of the 1950s through to Hudson's death in 1985 and beyond. Hudson's appearance in a series of adult comedies, starting with *Pillow Talk* in 1959, demarcates the final major phase of his film career. During this time, his position as the ideal middle-class man and the exemplar of suburban values is fully established and further entrenched, particularly as he made the transition from film star to television actor in the 1970s.

This chapter also examines how Hudson's work became noticeably darker as the 1960s came to an end. This process began with John Frankenheimer's *Seconds* in 1966, often critically regarded as one of his best dramatic performances, but can also be seen in his most extreme foray into the world of adult comedy: namely, Roger Vadim's *Pretty Maids All in a Row* (1971). Hudson's career ended on a particularly dark note when, after the public disclosure of his AIDS diagnosis and subsequent death in 1985, the star's reputation inevitably became entangled in wider debates around gay visibility and the social responsibilities of gay personalities. This chapter concludes with a postscript discussing the reappraisal (and revisionism) of Hudson's star image following his death and his appropriation as an object of critical enquiry by queer theorists. An example of this queer 'repurposing' of Hudson is Mark Rappaport's 'documentary' *Rock Hudson's Home Movies*, in which the actor's performances were purposefully reappropriated and re-read.

The sex comedies

When Ross Hunter presented Hudson with a treatment for a new comedy with the suggestive title *Pillow Talk* in 1959, the actor initially rejected it out of hand. Hunter persisted, however, and, following a reading of the final screenplay at his insistence, Hudson changed his mind despite some continuing reservations that the story was too 'racy' and the role of playboy Brad Allen was at variance with his carefully crafted public image. No doubt Hudson felt uneasy about the prospect of working in an unfamiliar genre and he reputedly needed a considerable amount of persuasion, not just from Hunter but also from his co-producer Marty Melcher and co-star Doris Day (Davidson and Hudson 1986: 112–14). He needn't have hesitated. When it was released in October 1959, *Pillow Talk* proved a huge commercial hit, winning an Academy Award for Best Screenplay, along with a further four Oscar nominations, including Doris Day as Best Actress and Thelma Ritter as Best Supporting Actress. As Steven Cohan observes, the film 'glamorized the star persona of Doris Day and established Rock Hudson as a romantic comedian on a par with Cary Grant' (1997: 265).

The success of *Pillow Talk* resulted in two subsequent Hudson–Day collaborations, *Lover Come Back* (1961) and *Send Me No Flowers* (1964). The 'Doris Day and Rock Hudson' sex comedies were a career-defining moment for both actors. While Day was transformed from a star of Hollywood musicals, Hudson's orbit shifted from romantic drama to romantic comedy. Moreover, Day and Hudson became the two most successful comic actors of the period and the very embodiment of the era's contemporary middle- class social and sexual values. The Day–Hudson trilogy initiated an especially productive period for both actors, one that resulted in several more sex comedies with other partners. However, these are typically overlooked in favour of the Day–Hudson films, which are widely regarded as epitomising the work of both actors at this time, even acting as a

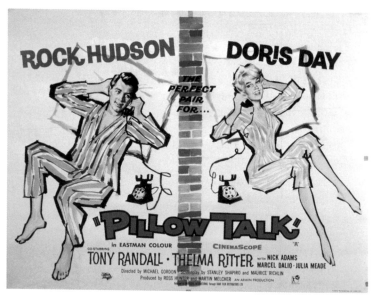

Poster for the phenomenally successful *Pillow Talk* (1959)

shorthand for a particular type of comedy from a specific historical and cultural moment. It has also become commonplace to deride these same comedies for their anachronistic worldview and clichéd gender roles. This kind of dismissive appraisal, however, tends to disregard social and cultural context, on the one hand, and ignore contemporary reception, on the other (for example, failing to note that *Pillow Talk* and *Lover Come Back* were both nominated for Best Screenplay, with *Pillow Talk* winning the Oscar). However, in more recent times several film scholars have recognised these films as culturally significant and much more nuanced than the standard account has allowed by attending closely to their textual details.[2]

The films demanded a new performance style from Hudson and film critic Bosley Crowther, writing in the *New York Times* in

1959, admired the 'surprising dexterity' with which Rock Hudson transformed himself into an urbane, elegant and polished comedy actor (1959: 24). Thirty years later, film historians Bruce Babbington and Peter Evans noted that, during the late 1950s and early 60s, 'the initially simple Hudson persona was continually added to, with his more multi-levelled parts discovering and defining aspects in him that could feed into later [...] roles' (1989: 204). In this way, Hudson was already being primed, albeit unwittingly, for a subsequent reinvention as a popular television actor. Of course, as I have argued in earlier chapters, his apparent naturalness and lightness of touch shown in the sex comedies was born out of determination, practice and collaborative work. Hudson claimed, for instance, that he learned how to perform as a comedy actor by watching Doris Day. Day was an experienced comic actress by this time and Hudson gained considerably from studying her technique, particularly in terms of tempo and timing, as well as the nuances of gesture and physicality, in effect learning his craft from an expert.

It is generally the case that, on the rare occasions when Hudson as an actor has been the subject of scholarship, it has almost always been within the context of a discussion of romantic comedy, most often in association with Doris Day and almost invariably in relation to *Pillow Talk*. The best examples include the work of Tamar Jeffers McDonald and Richard Dyer. In particular Jeffers McDonald has revealed the dynamics of the on-screen chemistry between Day and Hudson in an especially detailed reading of *Pillow Talk* as part of her forensic analyses of Doris Day's performances in *Doris Day Confidential: Hollywood, Sex and Stardom* (2013). In a much earlier essay, 'Very Little Wrist Movement': Rock Hudson Acts Out Sexual Heterodoxy' (2006), she also paid specific attention to Hudson's enactment of both the womaniser and the playboy, convincingly arguing that his performances of masculinity in all of the sex comedies of this period are ultimately undermined and unpicked in the unfolding of each film's narrative. Jeffers McDonald's research offers a rich appraisal of

Hudson's work, providing clear evidence that his signification and performance style in the Hudson–Day comedies is anything but a simplistic reproduction of dominant models of manhood and that these films articulate ambivalent and uncertain constructions of masculinity. Similarly, Richard Dyer had previously observed that:

These ... comedies have a reputation for blandness and safeness, for conventional sexual morality crossed with a complacent view of sex roles. Now they look much more interesting, bristling with sexual hysteria and gender confusion, more aware than they've been given credit for, of the instabilities of heterosexuality and normality. (2001: 166)

As important as *Pillow Talk*, *Lover Come Back* or *Send Me No Flowers* are in terms of Hudson's mature stardom, other sex comedies are just as significant but have received very little in the way of academic attention to date. These include *A Very Special Favor* (1965), made in the wake of the collaborations with Doris Day, and *Pretty Maids All in a Row*, the final sex comedy to feature Hudson and one that illustrates the trajectory of the genre as the 1960s gave way to the 70s.

Contexts for the sex comedy: masculinity in 'crisis' and the 'career woman'

The series of sex comedies that Hudson and Day popularised at the end of the 1950s and into the 60s emerged within the context of an increasingly sexualised American culture. This is a seeming paradox, given that the standard account of the 1950s is as a decade of conservatism and sexual repression, often incorrectly stereotyped for a 'static, conformist and pathological view of sex' (Jeffers McDonald: 2013: 29). It is, however, as Jeffers McDonald goes on to note, rather more accurate to regard this period as one in which there was a vigorous and widespread debate around gender roles, with a concomitant and heated discussion around sex and sexuality.

The popularisation of Freud's ideas in America, that began after his visit of 1909 and became fully entrenched by the 1940s, meant that sexuality and its relationship to neurosis had become part of popular discourse by the middle of the twentieth century.[3] The publication of the Kinsey reports in 1948 and 1953 (both bestsellers) placed sex and sexuality at the front and centre of popular debate.[4] So, as Barbara Klinger observes, by the middle of the 1950s, 'The Kinsey reports, *Playboy*, the publication of "adult" novels and suggestive paperbacks and exposé magazines like *Confidential* … foreground sex and sexual behaviour as very much part of the public cultural landscape' (1994: 53).

As detailed in Chapter 1, models of masculinity were also redrawn and redefined in America after World War II and this in turn contributed to a wider, if ill-defined, sense that manhood was in some way under threat or compromised by the nature of modern society and the corporate world in particular. These concerns were expressed, for example, in work as disparate as the sociological studies of Riesman, Glazer and Denney (*The Lonely Crowd: A Study of the Changing American Character*, 1950), Wright Mills's *White Collar: The American Middle Classes* (1951) and in popular fiction, such as Sloan Wilson's novel *The Man in the Gray Flannel Suit* (1955), made into a film in 1956. This sense of angst was to be summed up (and given a name) by political historian Arthur Schlesinger, Jr in an essay in *Esquire* magazine in 1958 entitled 'The Crisis of American Masculinity', a year prior to *Pillow Talk*'s release. In the essay, the title of which has become emblematic of popular opinion at the time, Schlesinger opines, 'What has happened to the American male? […] Today men are more and more conscious of maleness not as a fact but as a problem' (2008: 292). Schlesinger reveals his hand (and his reactionary politics) very quickly, informing us that 'the American woman meanwhile takes over more and more of the big decisions' (ibid.) and that 'women seem an expanding and aggressive force' and, even more alarmingly, for the author and assumed reader 'that this is an age of sexual ambiguity' (ibid.: 293). Regardless of the rather arcane prejudices on display in his essay, it's an important document in that it articulates a prevalent attitude, as James Gilbert notes, 'that conformity is emasculating and that modern mass society is feminizing' (2005: 63).

Concomitant with this sense that traditional masculinity was being undermined, two publications of the early 1960s stand as exemplars of the febrile nature of gender and sexual politics at this time. The first is Helen Gurley Brown's *Sex and the Single Girl: The Unmarried Woman's Guide to Men, Careers, the Apartment, Diet, Fashion, Money and Men*, published in 1962. Written by the editor of *Cosmopolitan*, the book caused a sensation and became an immediate bestseller. In the face of received wisdom and convention, Gurley Brown advocated (indeed, insisted upon) sex before marriage and provided a detailed manual on how to live the life of a career woman and attract men in the process. For contemporary readers, the author's 'philosophy' may seem cynical, with its emphasis on money, maintaining a good figure and an impeccably groomed appearance, all in the service of appealing to the opposite sex. Nonetheless, the heart of her message was both modern and one that her readership was keen to hear, particularly her observation that 'the single woman, far from being a creature to be pitied and patronized is emerging as the newest glamour girl of our times' (1962: 21).

A year later, Betty Friedan published *The Feminine Mystique*. Whereas Gurley Brown's book was populist in tone and content, *The Feminine Mystique* aimed to be a more serious exploration of the condition of American women and it echoed in many ways the sense of uncertainty and lack of fulfilment articulated by *The Lonely Crowd* and *The Man in the Gray Flannel Suit*. In an especially melodramatic passage, Friedan advises us: 'Each suburban wife struggled with it alone. As she ... lay beside her husband at night, she was afraid to ask even of herself the silent question, "Is this all?"' (1963: 11). Notwithstanding the examples of purple prose, the book is a systematic critique of women's place in modern society and implicitly rejects Gurley Brown's trite prescription of, in essence, sex and shopping. It is hard to overstate the significance of *The Feminine Mystique* in shaping what was to become Second Wave Feminism and although, in comparison, Gurley Brown's book seems vacuous, to say the least, both works confirm the fact that gender boundaries were being redrawn, with widespread uncertainty around what it meant to be a woman or a man at the time.[5] As part of this, the value and function of masculinity in the new managerial culture were being questioned just as women were increasingly rejecting 'traditional' gender roles. These developments go hand in hand with contemporaneous debates taking place in the popular press about 'hen-pecked' emasculated men and expressions of concern about the encroaching 'threat' of homosexuality.[6]

These cultural dilemmas around sex and gender form the backdrop for the Day and Hudson sex comedies. Doris Day (and subsequent actors such as Paula Prentiss, Leslie Caron, Gina Lollobrigida and Claudia Cardinale) are commonly positioned as Gurley Brown's 'single girls' (usually without the sex), while Hudson tends to be presented as the conflicted modern man performing a masculinity that is often the trigger for the working out of sexual dilemmas. In many if not all of the sex comedies, it is apparent that Hudson is cast in the role of a man who is 'acting out' masculinity in some way, either through subterfuge, masquerade (as in *Pillow Talk* and *Lover Come Back*) or by failing to live up to the masculine standard of the period (as in *Send Me No Flowers* and *Man's Favorite Sport?* [1964]). His function within the narrative is often to play the part of a man negotiating and 'working through' ascribed models of manhood and, in so doing, parodying them and drawing attention to their artifice. So, once again, Hudson's performances, so often dismissed as risible, unproblematic reproductions of hegemonic masculinity, reveal themselves as complicated iterations of wider anxieties. As Babbington and Evans have observed: 'It is notable how often the actor, whom his greatest director, Sirk, saw as definitively monolithic, is, to the contrary, cast in roles that revolve around his pretence that he is someone he is not' (1989: 206).

Furthermore, as will be discussed later, it has become routine to suggest that the details of Hudson's 'secret' private life and his hidden homosexuality were scrupulously suppressed from the general public. However, in the sex comedies of this later phase of his career, Hudson would often play parts in which his sexuality was routinely subjected to close scrutiny.

Middle-class taste, the ideal husband and the eligible bachelor

At the same time as summoning up and articulating some of the contemporaneous fears of the consequences for the status quo of the new career woman and the white-collar male, the sex comedies also, paradoxically, worked to construct an ideal of middle-class metropolitan (and suburban) affluence. The fairly consistent charges of complacency and conservatism made against the sex comedies are undeniably concerned with their settings, milieu and implied politics. Apparently motivated by wider social anxieties, the films paradoxically valorise the consumerism and middle-class value systems that precipitate the same fears. This is perhaps not surprising given that, as Janet McCracken notes, consumerism was often posited as the solution to problems and the antidote to anxiety and neurosis during the 1950s.

As long as there was a genuine hope of widespread economic prosperity ... women worked and waited. This faith in economic salvation from their suffering allowed the women of this generation to bear their conflicted inner life with relative serenity and grace. (2001: 261)

Hudson's considerable triumphs in the sex-comedy genre can thus be attributed in no small part to his ability to embody, largely through his physical appearance, middle-class values and middle-class taste. In the aftermath of his success in *Magnificent Obsession*, his image became increasingly refined during the second half of the 1950s. With his physical stature, symmetrical features, dark wavy hair and immaculate grooming, Hudson conformed to Anglo/American standards of male beauty. He is not, for example, the epicene type epitomised by Rudolph Valentino or Ramon Navarro in the 1920s and 30s, whose looks spoke of otherness, sexuality and the threat of both. Instead, Hudson is the square-jawed, all American, 'boy-next-door' type, in the mould of (and belonging to a lineage that includes) Gary Cooper and Joel McCrea. Even as Hudson moved into this more mature stage of his career, his looks continue to play a part in his evolving star persona and his ongoing popularity. Indeed, 'looking like Rock Hudson' would become shorthand for someone possessing male sex appeal.

Hudson was no different from other actors of his generation in that the studios expected him to promote himself and his films by starring in commercials. The scope and range of commodities that Hudson advertised illustrate his assumed attraction to middle-class suburban audiences. Hudson's perfectly groomed and tailored appearance meant that he was used by clothing manufacturers, such as menswear company Hart Schaffner & Marx and Jockey (a famous advertisement of 1963 bears the legend 'This is Rock Hudson's foot') as well as Gillette. He also promoted car manufacturers, such as Chrysler, and various airlines. His most high-profile campaign though was as the spokesman for Camel cigarettes. The *mise en scène* of the Camel advertisements often foregrounds Hudson's outdoors appeal, (they were frequently set in 'manly' looking dens), his easy masculinity and relaxed and unthreatening persona.[7] Hudson was positioned as the epitome of the modern man in these advertisements and this was reflected more generally in the way that he was represented across various media. For example, in an article in *Life* magazine in December 1956, a 'survey' reveals that popular singer Perry Como was identified as the 'ideal husband' of twenty year olds, alongside other equally eligible public figures, including William Holden, Tony Curtis, Elvis Presley, John F. Kennedy and Rock Hudson. The qualities enumerated as prerequisites for a husband encompassed some clearly associated with Hudson (such as sincerity, honesty and a lack of egotism) and some that he did not possess (namely, a college education, the desire for a large family). Nonetheless, Hudson's inclusion on the list speaks to the perception within American popular culture that he was marriageable material. A year earlier, for example, Hudson had appeared on the cover of *Life* with the strapline of 'Hollywood's most handsome bachelor'. It is notable that there is a duality in the representation of Hudson in the press coverage of the period as either a potential husband or a free-spirited bachelor, and this was subsequently to map on to his later parts in the sex comedies.[8] This shifting between the role of the idealised suburban husband and the bachelor/playboy in fact runs through the cycle of sex comedies and is to mark out the trajectory from the relative innocence of *Pillow Talk* to the darkness of *Pretty Maids All in a Row*.

A Very Special Favor (Michael Gordon, 1965)

Directed by Michael Gordon, *A Very Special Favor* is not singled out for study with anything like the same frequency as the films of the Hudson–Day trilogy. Gordon, who had directed *Pillow Talk*, continued to work with Hudson and Day as well as directing comparable sex comedies with actors such as Kim Novak (*Boys Night*

Out [1962]) and Kirk Douglas (*For Love or Money* [1963]). His career was resuscitated by *Pillow Talk*[9] and he was to acknowledge, no doubt with some gratitude, that the success of the film was in part due to Day's perfectionism, necessitating extensive rehearsals. He also regarded Hudson as an actor who was 'serious' about his work (Davis 2005: 212). In the film, Hudson demonstrates his comedy skills as a playboy masquerading as an 'impaired' modern man in order to bring a career woman to her senses. Moreover, in the role of Paul Chadwick, Hudson simultaneously endorses and satirises the masculine persona that his stardom is predicated on, and which became the hallmark of his performances during this period. As a comic actor, it is notable that Hudson proved adept at sending up the same ideal of masculinity that his star persona so insistently asserted.

The film is the story of estranged father Frenchman Michel Boullard (Charles Boyer) enlisting American businessman and playboy Chadwick to seduce his daughter, psychoanalyst and controlling career woman Lauren Boullard (Leslie Caron), who has chosen an unsuitable, passive, feminised (and 'hen-pecked') fiancé in Arnold Plum (Dick Shawn). Through a typically labyrinthine set of narrative twists and turns, Chadwick sets out to deceive Lauren by posing as a patient and claiming to be developing a phobia of the women who relentlessly pursue him. Chadwick ultimately realises that he is falling in love with the very woman that he was persuaded to fool. Consequently, as in both *Pillow Talk* and *Lover Come Back*, Hudson is cast as the playboy trickster whose plots and schemes result in his undoing, culminating in his romantic union with the female lead. Simultaneously, the narrative situates a career woman's professional success as a problem that needs to be resolved (as in *Pillow Talk* before it). Hudson's playboy is a disruptive figure, yet he is also offered as the solution to the 'problem' of a woman whose career ambitions have alienated her from sanctioned feminine norms (passivity, emotionality and so on). The figure of the playboy was by no means a new phenomenon; indeed it had taken hold in the US by this time due to *Playboy* magazine (launched in 1953), a publication firmly embedded in popular culture by the mid-1960s. The magazine and the iconography of the playboy both connected sex, conspicuous consumption and a certain lifestyle, detached from the pressures of matrimony and suburban middle-class respectability.[10] A figure of envy to some, the playboy was also regarded with a degree of ambivalence. As Claire Mortimer observes in *Romantic Comedy*,

The playboy is a threat to social equilibrium who needs to be cut down to size and integrated into society. He is a fantasy figure, with his enviable lifestyle and dedication to pleasure, yet the audience can feel gratification, as the playboy is normalised at the end of the film, with marriage and children. (2010: 50)

The film's title sequence produces the *mise en scène* of playboy luxury in highly stylised form. Silver-topped canes, along with surprisingly suggestive champagne corks popping into glasses, set a daring tone, one already established in the earlier sex comedies and the standard register for these productions by 1965. *A Very Special Favor* is lavishly mounted with no expense spared in terms of location shooting as well as John McCarthy and John Austin's luxurious set designs, just as in the Ross Hunter-produced *Pillow Talk* six years earlier. Stanley Shapiro (one of the scriptwriters of the Oscar-winning *Pillow Talk*) had become a producer in his own right by the time of this production and went on to make *That Touch of Mink* with Doris Day in 1962.

A Very Special Favor opens in Paris. Hudson's Paul Chadwick is an executive, described as a 'troubleshooter sent in to assess critical situations', who has won a legal case against Michel Boullard. As will be discovered later, the assignation of the title of troubleshooter becomes significant on more than one front but, at this stage, it situates him as professional, confident and affluent. He is also established from the outset as a playboy seducer. The opening scene follows shots of an open-topped sports car racing along the Seine and past the Eiffel Tower to the courtroom. Chadwick is seen performing his seduction technique on a beautiful blonde Frenchwoman (who it transpires is the judge in the case that he wins), while two elderly American tourists watch on with a mixture of envy and disgust. The scene sets Chadwick up as a smooth and manipulative trickster and Hudson, who has by now refined this routine in six previous sex comedies, parodies his star persona as the glamorous and romantic bachelor. His seemingly attentive manner and soft deep voice is suggestive of a seduction that is undermined, for comic intent, by his gaze into the far distance over the shoulder of his partner while he goes through the motions.

From this opening sequence, Hudson is identified as both the star of the film and, just as importantly, as the focus of admiration (with some degree of erotic investment) for the rest of the supporting cast. Hudson's Chadwick is a man that women find irresistible and, consequently, men envy (even Frenchmen, stereotyped as the experts in such matters here). So, for instance, on the return flight to New York, a female passenger serves Chadwick and Boullard drinks as a pretext to offer the former keys to her apartment. Later, at the airport, Chadwick simultaneously phones two girls from two phone booths to arrange dates. When Boullard arrives at Chadwick's apartment to persuade him to seduce his daughter, he is presented with the spectacle of a succession of somnambulant women obsessed with Chadwick, taking away his laundry or cleaning his apartment as a result of their romantic fixation. The seemingly casual misogyny of these details is undeniably jarring for a contemporary audience, especially given that the assumed primary audience for this material would have been female. Just as jarring is Boyer's claim that the career woman is the genesis of all societal problems and the reason for emasculated American men as well as dissolute playboys such as Chadwick. These contemporary reservations aside, Hudson's performance of the skilled seducer, manipulator and charmer is finely tuned. He plays Chadwick with more than a touch of satire,

Paul Chadwick (Hudson) 'performs' emotional
trauma in *A Very Special Favor* (1965)

as a character who uses his charms as if it were second nature, while delivering his insincere romantic lines as if reading advertising copy.

The primary motivation for Boullard's desire to intervene in his daughter's life is concern that her fiancé Arnold Plum is inadequate. Boullard meets Plum in his daughter's waiting room and Shawn's performance sets him up as the antithesis of Hudson's suave masculine seducer. In a scene overplayed for comic effect, Shawn sits with his legs crossed in what is meant to be read as an effeminate manner. He twitches, is overly chatty and is in effect playing the fretful 'wife' to Caron's domineering and controlling 'husband'; the role reversal here is the indicator that the relationship is doomed and that Hudson's unassailable masculinity is needed to restore order. Shawn then assumes the 'comic' male role, previously played by Tony Randall to Hudson's straight man in *Pillow Talk* and *Lover Come Back*.

Chadwick is persuaded to take on the challenge of impersonating a weakened male in order to fool (and subsequently seduce) Caron's character, with inevitably complicated results. The film is a showcase for Hudson's developed range of comic registers. He is required to play the smooth and insincere predator, the trickster, acting out the part of a vulnerable and insecure man who is not only confused by women but also afraid of his appeal to them. His performances in the psychiatrist's chair are especially effective, not least because they demand swift and subtle shifts in pacing, tone and physicality. Hudson shows himself to be especially adept at these micro-performative details, shifting from a heightened tone to a more muted and naturalistic one. For instance, in a scene in which he reveals the extent of his psychological distress, he stands up, moves away from Caron, drawing on the rhetoric of melodrama by gazing through venetian blinds to recount the tragic tale of 'Wanda', the girl who caused his problems with women, even covering his face with his hands for comic effect when lying. He then quickly shifts registers, adopting a more naturalistic tone for the deadpan delivery of the ironic punchline, 'Do you know what it feels like to be wanted just for your body?' The homosexual subtext that has sometimes been noted in Hudson's sex comedies (usually in the relationship between Hudson's and Tony Randall's characters) is here brought to the surface. It resurfaces again towards the end of *A Very Special Favor*, which involves a final ruse where Lauren rushes to 'rescue' Chadwick from a homosexual liaison at a motel. This, however, is yet another trick on Chadwick's part, as not only is he manifestly *not* a homosexual, his supposed 'gay lover' is a woman dressed in men's clothes.[11] The joke (unintentionally ironic, given future revelations) is that questioning Hudson's sexuality is inherently comic as we are completely assured through his appearance, demeanour and behaviour that the very last thing that he could possibly be is homosexual. In essence we trust and can depend on the certainty of who Hudson 'really' is.

This film cements Hudson's status as a major comic actor. Additionally, by this time, Hudson's star image had been so carefully constructed and his performance register so refined that the performance of heteromasculinity that he presented to audiences was immaculately polished. He was by now an unassailable paradigm of masculinity to such an extent that he could play a hypochondriac (*Send Me No Flowers*), a failed fisherman (*Man's Favorite Sport*) and even masquerade as a homosexual without compromising his credentials as the quintessence of normality.

Pretty Maids All in a Row (Roger Vadim, 1971)

In many respects, Roger Vadim's *Pretty Maids All in a Row* is the logical, if rather surprising, conclusion to the cycle of Hudson's sex comedies that began with *Pillow Talk*. It's also a film that demanded the casting of someone like Hudson, possessed of unassailable heterosexual credentials, in a pivotal role in order to work. The film was produced by MGM to fairly blatantly capitalise on the phenomenal success that Twentieth Century-Fox had enjoyed with the Russ Meyer extravaganza *Beyond the Valley of the Dolls* (1970).[12] Meyer's lurid sex, drugs and rock and roll melodrama had been met with a mixture of critical incomprehension and derision but had nonetheless made ten times its production budget at the box office. Vadim was a director routinely associated with scenes of nudity and sex in such controversial films as *And God Created Woman* (1956), starring his first wife Brigitte Bardot, and *Barbarella* (1968), starring his third wife Jane Fonda. As such, Vadim was an obvious choice for MGM's plan for a low-budget, sexually titillating money-spinner. The film was extensively promoted through a disparate range of media outlets, from *Playboy* (drawing attention to the sexual overtones of the film) to *Life* magazine, which included a picture feature of Hudson surrounded by an assortment of 'teenage beauties' (1970: 30). The poster for the release was redolently suggestive, stating: 'Roger Vadim, the director who uncovered Brigitte Bardot, Catherine Deneuve and Jane Fonda now brings you the American high school girl ... and Rock Hudson.'

It is interesting (and not a little ironic) to note that Hudson, so wary about being involved in the 'racy' *Pillow Talk* ten years earlier, enthusiastically embraced the part of 'Tiger' in the Vadim movie. This was his first R-rated venture and the first time that he had been cast in the role of an ambiguous antihero/villain. As Sara Davidson reports, he was thrilled with the prospect of playing the sex-crazed, psychopathic high-school counsellor declaring, 'I'm a murderer and a stud! I get to do everything' (Davidson and Hudson 1986: 168).

By contemporary standards, the film's problematic subject matter (teachers having sex with and then murdering their adolescent pupils) would scarcely be regarded as conventional comedy fare.[13] It is of course designed as a dark satire of the new, sexualised, post-1960s culture, but nonetheless still feels uncomfortably sexist and anachronistic to a modern audience. Set in the aftermath of the sexual revolution in California, the home of free love, the film perhaps suggests through its young protagonist something of the rather more prosaic reality of the experience of many during this supposedly permissive period. John David Carson plays Ponce, a schoolboy preoccupied with women's bodies, almost completely excluded from but desperately wanting to engage in a world of supposedly carefree sex. Ponce's naïve and inhibited desire is contrasted with Hudson's character's sexual sophistication (and depravity).

Hudson plays the school sports coach and counsellor, Michael 'Tiger' McDrew, who is fleetingly introduced in the opening scene, passionately kissing a nude schoolgirl in his counselling room, while the sex-obsessed Ponce discovers the body of one of Tiger's earlier victims in a bathroom stall. The scene suggests that Tiger's psychopathic sexual passions situate him as both absurdly insatiable and oblivious to the consequences of his actions. When police cars arrive at the school, the bare-chested counsellor, standing over the student he has presumably just had sex with, gazes out of the window at the unfolding drama seemingly perplexed by the crime scene that we already suspect is the result of his actions.

Hudson's casting here is inspired, capitalising on the personal charm that is central to his star persona, his status as the epitome of heteronormativity and his physical stature. By 1971, Hudson was forty-six years old and, while his physique is still athletic, he is clearly a middle-aged man by this time. As in earlier films, there are opportunities to regard his body as an erotic spectacle but the once-toned natural physique now has a looser aspect (e.g., his paunch). A beige wardrobe of fitted shirts and trousers, along with a moustache and longer hair, mark a departure from his usual meticulously groomed appearance, these being designed to suggest a charismatic and yet distinctly suburban apostle of free love and individualism. Tiger, we discover, is an advocate of limitless hedonism, telling one of his students not to read books, advising instead that 'an animal body needs animal exercise … . I'm gonna teach you how to live man, how to *feel*!' This hedonism, along with his excessive stamina and appetite, are presented as 'unnatural' or at least surprising for a man of his age. While counselling Ponce, Tiger greedily swallows bottles of coke and glasses of organic apple juice one after another with so much gusto that it seems disproportionate. Similarly, when Angie Dickinson's character (a new teacher) first visits Tiger in his office, he is seen balancing his weight on a makeshift seesaw, sliding precariously from side to side like a surfer. The athleticism of this exercise and the spectacle of Hudson performing it, shot from a low angle, is offset by the calm and relaxed tone of his voice. In a later scene with Dickinson, he fondles her breasts while explaining the differences between sex and seduction. The same calming bass vocal tones are contrasted with the physical performance of what amounts to a sexual assault. Hudson's distinctive vocal qualities are played with throughout the film. We discover, for example, that Tiger is writing a philosophical tract on pedagogy and his deep voice lends a comic gravitas to the recordings he makes for his manuscript. In a particularly striking moment, designed to express the callous nature of his psychopathology, we see him at home, dressed in a kaftan, dictating text for his book while watching TV news footage of the removal of one of his victims from a crime scene.

Hudson plays Tiger as an affable, likeable figure, a man whose status as teacher, counsellor and sports coach positions him as an object of admiration within the high-school setting as well as within the wider community. He belongs to the lineage of all Hudson's characters in the previous sex comedies, in that he possesses many of the most desirable and aspirational qualities of the modern American male: he is sporty, socially adept, handsome. He also has a young and beautiful wife (and a child) and he lives in a luxurious and modishly appointed beachfront home. This domesticity is presented in the film as something of a surprising aspect of the character's life. So, for example, after having sex with yet another student, he arrives home to see a beautiful woman walking past his house. The scene, played out in silence and through an exchange of glances and reaction shots, gives the impression that Tiger is about to pick up a woman on the street, even though, as the sequence concludes, she turns out to be his wife. In this short vignette, cinematic rhetoric and Hudson's character play with audience expectations at the same time that Tiger is playing with his wife. He is once again a trickster, a man acting a part to fool (primarily) women, only now he is not only an older trickster but his tricks have much more dangerous consequences. Hudson's decision to accept this role suggests that the actor was prepared to both expose his ageing process and take greater risks. This was potentially a much more hazardous undertaking than his roles at the start of the 1960s, one that not only departed from his established image but also provided a dark parody of his established persona. It also suggests that, in his mid-forties, the star was keen to extend his range.

The career strategies of a mature star

By 1970, Rock Hudson was no longer young and yet remained working in a profession in which being youthful supposedly carries a high premium. Indeed, one of the commonplace truisms so often repeated about Hollywood cinema is that it is an industry preoccupied with youth. For example, an article in *Photoplay* from the early 1920s vividly illustrates this perception, the writer observing that, 'In all the history of the world there was never a place where youth was so lavished with fame and fortune' (1925: 30).[14] However, as the industry developed during the course of the twentieth century, it became increasingly possible for stars (and in particular male stars) to retain their status as youth passed. As Edgar Morin suggested in *The Stars: An Account of the Star System in Motion Pictures*,

After 1930 we have the aging heroes of the middle-class theater in France (Victor Francen, Jean Murat), and after 1940, in Hollywood, the Clark Gables, Gary Coopers, Humphrey Bogarts, etc., begin new careers as "the men who have really lived.' (1961: 23)

Consequently, as Hudson moved into middle age during the late 1960s and early 70s, there were already precedents to indicate that he would be able to maintain a career *and* a profile as a star. He did so, moreover, by diversifying into other media (notably television), as well as by extending the range of material he was cast in. We can see this gradual process starting to take place by the middle of the 1960s, continuing through the 70s right the way through to the end of his career in 1985.

I would argue that there are a set of strategies that actors, their agents, producers and casting agents can adopt to effectively frame the career of an ageing star and, in Hudson's case, almost all of these strategies were deployed at various times. These can be described as parody and self-parody, nostalgia and recycling, character roles, expedience and 'challenging' roles.

Parody/self-parody

Older actors often take on roles that send up their star persona, drawing ironic attention to their image or the performative characteristics that their fame has become predicated upon. For example, Bette Davis and Joan Crawford in Robert Aldrich's tour de force *What Ever Happened to Baby Jane?* (1962), perform exaggerated caricatures of the capricious vixen in Davis's case and the suffering heroine in Crawford's. Hudson's work in the sex comedies began in *Pillow Talk* by poking a gentle finger at his performance as Bick Benedict in *Giant* and, as the 1960s progressed, the roles continued in this broadly parodic vein.

Nostalgia/recycling

Returning to and recycling previously successful formats that hark back to 'high points' are other common career-prolonging strategies. The most obvious example of this in Hudson's case (notwithstanding his foray into television melodrama with his performance as Daniel Reece in *Dynasty* [1981–9]), is the adaptation of Agatha Christie's *The Mirror Crack'd* (1980). In keeping with the customary 'star-studded' line-up of actors in Christie adaptations, the film casts Hudson alongside Elizabeth Taylor, Tony Curtis and Kim Novak in roles that remind audiences of their personas in their hey-day as major Hollywood stars during the 1950s. The film demands campy broad gestures from Taylor, Novak and Curtis, while requiring Hudson to reprise his muted performance register with a newer, sinister undercurrent.

Character roles

Some stars make a smooth transition from star status to character actor. Al Pacino, Robert De Niro and even Marlon Brando are all examples of actors who moved into character roles as they aged. This is perhaps the one strategy not apparent in Hudson's career. In part, at least, because his star persona was built around such a clearly determined sense of stability, the risk of disrupting or subverting that (together with the limits of his dramatic range) would not have made this viable.

Expedience

Inevitably, older actors have to accept roles in order to maintain a profile or indeed for financial reward alone. In the 1970s and 80s

Hudson had to make when these kinds of expedient choices, resulting in a mixture of the Western *Showdown* (1973), low-budget sci-fi/horror *Embryo* (1976), the disaster movie *Avalanche* (1978) and subsequent TV movies during the 1980s.

'Challenging' roles

The final strategy open to the ageing star is to take on what are often described and even marketed as 'challenging' roles. This largely suggests parts that stretch the perceived limits of an actor's dramatic range or shift a star's persona into new (and perhaps riskier) territory. In Hudson's case, this strategy is best exemplified by the John Frankenheimer film *Seconds*, which has been subject to one of the most surprising reappraisals since its release in 1966. Hudson's performance has in fact been a central factor in this critical revision of the film.

Seconds (John Frankenheimer, 1966)

Frankenheimer's *Seconds* bears all of the distinctive hallmarks of the director's authorship. The film is suspenseful and has the same paranoid, alienated atmosphere evident in *The Manchurian Candidate* (1962) as well as, to a lesser degree, in *Seven Days in May* (1964). By the mid-1960s, Frankenheimer had extensive experience of working with major Hollywood stars and, in particular, had an especially productive relationship with Burt Lancaster, resulting most famously in *Birdman of Alcatraz* (1962). While Frankenheimer had gained success in collaboration with Lancaster, his association with Hudson initially resulted in far fewer plaudits. The critical reception of *Seconds* on release was notoriously hostile. The film, nominated for the Palme D'Or in 1966, was booed by the audience at the end of the

James Wong Howe's endlessly inventive
camerawork for *Seconds* (1966)

screening in Cannes, to the surprise of director and star alike. Film
critics were no less scathing and the film proved a commercial
disaster. However, over the years, alongside a wider reevaluation of
John Frankenheimer's career more generally, the perception of
Seconds has shifted, from ostensibly that of a cult classic (its failure at
the box office and reviled critical reception positioning it as the *sine
qua non* of cult films in some quarters) to a more prominent place in
the director's oeuvre.

The film is not just interesting because of its shift in status or its
demonstration of Frankenheimer's directorial vision but also because
of its technical and visual innovations. James Wong Howe, who had
lit Clara Bow in the 1920s and used helicopters for the first time for
the aerial shots in *Picnic* (1955), was the director of photography and
his extensive use of wide-angle and (most notably) fish-eye lenses,
handheld camera, as well as low-key, monochrome photography
enhance the dystopian atmosphere of the film.[15]

Seconds is the story of Arthur Hamilton (John Randolph), a
bored middle-aged businessman who decides to give up his suburban

existence and buy a new life and identity from a shadowy Kafkaesque corporation that arranges his death and rebirth following surgery as the 'second' Antioch 'Tony' Wilson (Rock Hudson), an artist with a seemingly perfect life. He quickly realises that this new idyll is no less of a trap than his previous suburban existence and he tries to return to his old life, with disastrous consequences. It is a film that very explicitly deals with the anxieties of middle age and with the social roles and expectations that come with maturity and responsibility. It is, in effect, a fantasy about escape and the attendant consequences of attempting to fulfil that fantasy.

The film is unlike any project that Hudson had been involved in until this point and gave the actor one of his most unique roles. He is often described in popular accounts as playing 'against type' in *Seconds* but this characterisation is inaccurate as, in fact, he is cast as the all too familiar character of the wealthy, handsome 'bachelor'. The difference between this and previous versions is that the idealised vision of glamour, wealth and privilege associated with him in the sex comedies is seen as empty, alienating and dystopian in *Seconds*. Scenes in which we see the immaculately groomed Hudson being served dinner by his butler in silence or walking along the beach in splendid isolation seem to explicitly undermine the consumerist dreams of the Hudson and Day comedies.

Hudson was by no means Frankenheimer's first choice (he had been in discussions with Laurence Olivier about the part) as he was apparently considered too 'glamorous' (Barton Palmer 2010: 56). Notwithstanding this compromise in casting decisions, Frankenheimer, like almost all Hudson's directors, admired his work ethic but, nonetheless, was to repeatedly claim (rather ungenerously) that, despite probably representing the actor's best work (describing it as a 'gutsy, honest, marvellous performance'), it was also, paradoxically, the reason why the film flopped (Armstrong 2013: 77). In short, Hudson brought with him a set of generic expectations that audiences were not ready or even willing to have challenged. This casting is nonetheless crucial to the artistic, if not the commercial, success of the project. As Steven Farber, in *Film Quarterly*, observes in one of the less critical listings:

I'd say Frankenheimer quite ingeniously cast Rock Hudson as the new Hamilton. Pauline Kael writes in protest, 'It is a horror picture: imagine having a second chance at life and coming back as Rock Hudson!' Well, that's the point, Hudson is meant to suggest all of the hollow youthfulness and handsomeness that we wish for ourselves in our wispiest daydreams. (1966–7: 26)

Having turned forty-one in 1966 and therefore scarcely 'youthful', Hudson played the 'second' of John Randolph's Arthur Hamiltons, who was fifty-one. Initial casting discussions took place on the basis that Hudson would play both parts but Frankenheimer and Hudson soon agreed that another actor should take the Arthur Hamilton role, enhancing the dramatic impact of Hudson's 'reveal' following surgery forty minutes into the film. Frankenheimer decided on an unknown, selecting Randolph. Hudson's performance then was designed to be that of a middle-aged man reborn in the body of a younger man. The narrative thus makes quite particular demands on both actors. Randolph needs to convey the middle-aged ennui of someone marooned in a sexless and empty marriage, detached from his environment, while Hudson's task is, to a large extent, to reproduce the tone and style of Randolph's performance, building his own performance out of this initial alienated figure. The actors spent a significant period of time in pre-production shadowing each other in order to imitate each other's mannerisms and physicality. Frankenheimer was able to exploit Hudson's archetypically suave star image and, in turn, Hudson proved himself capable of enacting someone inhabiting (and ultimately trapped within) this glamorous star body, who quickly comes to recognise the hollow ideals behind this dream of escape. The shifts in tone and pacing required are considerable, with Hudson exploiting his full range, playing Tony in

John Randolph and Hudson in *Seconds* (1966)

a variety of attitudes: isolated and bored by the empty luxury surrounding him; inhibited and angered by the confusing morals and behaviours of his fellow 'seconds'; inebriated and then regretful when he begins to realise the errors of his choice; and, finally, anxious and afraid as he tries to return to his previous life.

The film is frequently framed in close-up, some of the handheld camerawork feeling voyeuristic and intrusive. In a short sequence on a plane following his transformative surgery, Hudson reacts to a voiceover explaining his new life of freedom, the very thing that 'every middle aged man in America would like to have'. His face is shot in profile, to draw attention to his famed 'film-star looks' yet what it conveys is neither pleasure nor self-satisfaction but instead a mixture of loneliness and fear. His arrival at his new home and introduction to his butler is largely shot from behind, so that the audience feel they are following him. Hudson's reactions are key to creating the sense of atmosphere, given that his dialogue is minimal and the scenes structured to be unnerving, with camerawork alternating from low-angle to point-of-view shots. Hudson's performance is still and contained, his voice faltering and tripping over words, his movements around his new home slow and deliberate.

Tony's isolation is disrupted by the introduction of Nora (Salome Jens), who he encounters at the beach and subsequently becomes romantically involved with. Jens is tellingly styled to remind audiences of Doris Day and the vivacity of her performance equally bears some similarities. The on-screen chemistry between the two protagonists, however, could scarcely be more different. Whereas Jens's Nora embodies an unsettling energy (she is also positioned as exotic thanks to a faint 'European' accent), Hudson's Tony is cold and detached. At the conclusion of their first meeting and without any obvious motivation, Nora runs recklessly into the sea with an energy that seems hysterical, while Tony watches, impassive and expressionless. Unlike the teasing banter that marked Day and

Hudson relations, here there are stilted silences and a palpable sense of social awkwardness. As a result of their meeting, Tony invites himself to a 'gathering' that Nora is attending in Santa Barbara which, it soon transpires, is a Bacchanalian orgy complete with pan pipes, wine-treading and gratuitous nudity. While Jens's character throws herself into the spirit of the event (not something one could possibly imagine Day doing), stripping and enthusiastically joining in nude grape-treading, Hudson portrays Tony as the inhibited, middle-aged Hamilton inside Tony's body. He looks uncomfortable and the increasingly frenetic camerawork exaggerates his disorientation and discomfort and final, hysterical, submission to the orgiastic ritual.

This 'descent' into hedonism is followed by a party sequence which ultimately triggers Tony's realisation that he wants to return to suburban normality. In the scene, Tony's drunkenness becomes increasingly reckless and disruptive. Frankenheimer and Hudson both claimed that the actor had to get genuinely drunk for the scene, which is lengthy and disturbing. Wong Howe uses a camera fastened to Hudson's back, delivering a queasy sense of intoxication, while big close-ups provide an intrusive subjectivity by focusing on the microperformative details of the acting.

Tony's illicit visit to his wife from his previous life, following this nightmarish party, becomes the trigger for the film's denouement. Here Hudson reprises the stillness and composure that was established at the start of the film in a scene with elaborately composed static compositions, such as one in which his wife reminisces about her husband being a 'quiet man' while Hudson sits in studied silence shot in close-up. Following this interlude, Tony is returned to the company to await the operation that will restore him to his old life. This leads into the final scenes in which the bedbound Tony submits to his fate and is wheeled into surgery for a conclusion that we understand as his death. This final sequence is surprising in its affective power and is truly frightening.

Tony Antioch (Hudson) revisits his wife from
his previous life in *Seconds* (1966)

This is in no small part due to the shock impact of witnessing the
romantic heartthrob of 1950s Hollywood, gagged and strapped to a
gurney, screaming in terror. This final sequence lasts just over five
minutes and its close-ups on the bound and incapacitated Hudson
alternate with point-of-view shots. In these closing minutes we
vividly see Hudson's commitment to the role, shifting his
performance from confusion to blind panic and, most shockingly, to
teary oblivion. The distorted camerawork emphasises the disturbing
aspect, focusing almost exclusively on Hudson. As Vivien Sobchack
notes, the use of fish-eye lenses here represents 'not the real world
but the subjective insight of a beaten man, overwhelmed by
irresistible diabolic strength' (2001: 131).

Seconds is a film that might, retrospectively, seem prescient in
its implicit dismantling of the myth of Rock Hudson's glamorous
image. Indeed, some critics have suggested that there is a queer
subtext to the film, in its story of a middle-aged man's secret desire
to free himself from the shackles of suburban respectability and
heteronormativity. Rebecca Bell-Metereau, for example, argues that

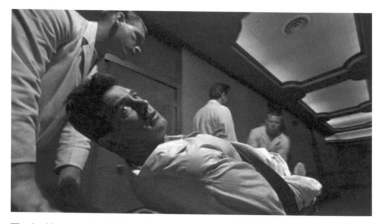

The shocking spectacle of Hudson, the
glamorous playboy strapped to a gurney at the
end of *Seconds* (1966)

'Hudson displays a keen sensitivity to the plight of a character living
a lie in order to achieve his dream' (2011: 57). However, what the
film most clearly demonstrates is the level of complexity Hudson
brought to this role and how this often manifests itself most
effectively through subtlety and nuance rather than broad gesture.
As David Sterritt observes, in *Seconds*, 'Hudson's performance is the
most skilful and courageous of his career' (2011: 28).

Rock Hudson's 'second' life

Unlike many of his Hollywood contemporaries, the decline of the
studio system did not spell the end of Hudson's stardom as he forged
a successful second career as a TV actor. This was, however, very
obviously a career choice motivated by expediency in the first
instance and fashioned around the recycling of past roles and
triumphs rather than establishing new ground. Hudson was no

stranger to television. During his rise to stardom in the early 1950s he had featured in commercials on a regular basis, advertising cars and shaving products. In 1955, he made a guest appearance as himself in an episode of *I Love Lucy* and, in 1959, he was the star of *The Big Party by Revlon*, a glamorous extravaganza, alongside co-star Tallulah Bankhead and guest star Sammy Davis, Jr. While TV spots became part of the marketing strategy of stars during the 1950s and into the 60s, Hudson made little secret of his low opinion of the medium and only moved into television acting begrudgingly after the highly publicised flop *Darling Lili* (1970), in which he was cast with Julie Andrews (Kalfatovic 2001: 417).

McMillan & Wife (1971–7)

In September 1971, Hudson starred in a feature-length pilot for a new NBC series called *McMillan & Wife* that ran in rotation with *Columbo* (1971–2003) and *McCloud* (1970–7) as part of NBC's *Mystery Movie* series. The show would become one of the most successful television series of the 1970s and secure Hudson's popularity as a television personality, based on the same unassuming natural manliness that had been the hallmark of his star persona during his Hollywood years. The series was frequently (and often disparagingly) compared to Dashiell Hammett's *The Thin Man* series of books, subsequently made into films in the 1930s and a television series in the 50s. In fact, Hammett's Nick and Nora Charles bear only a passing resemblance to Stuart and Sally McMillan, and the chief conceit of the series (that the male protagonist is drawn unwillingly into solving crimes uncovered by his wife) is the principal similarity. The show's mixture of crime/mystery and light comedy was a natural extension of Hudson's work in the sex comedies of the 1960s. It is notable that Hudson, whose career was distinguished by collaborative pairings with female actors who were often older than him, was in his mid-forties by 1971 and at this stage cast alongside a much younger actress. He is in effect the 'sexy older man', who is virile enough to attract an equally sexy (as well as quirky and vivacious) wife in her twenties. The actress in this case was Susan Saint James, who secured the role after consideration was given to both Jill Clayburgh and (tellingly, given her future roles with Woody Allen) Diane Keaton.

While the show was a major hit, Hudson's attitude to *McMillan & Wife* was ambivalent from beginning to end. In 1972, in a syndicated question-and-answer feature article supposedly 'written' by Hudson (though clearly prepared by the Universal Studios press department), he discusses the differences between acting for the big and small screens. Hudson is described as the 'major motion picture star' who has 'been one of the few to make the transition from one dramatic medium to another with happy results all round' (Hudson 1972: 23). For Hudson, there are obvious technical differences between television and film, often revolving around the scale of gesture required. He notes, somewhat ruefully that, 'For the tiny screen you have to punch up your work. You can't underplay as I would in a movie' (ibid.).

As the show was moving towards the end of its run in the late 1970s, Hudson would speak once again about his career, past and present. In 1976, for example, another syndicated article asked 'Did Rock Hudson Become a Star before He Became an Actor?' (1976: 2). The article (an interview again) returns to the seemingly perennial topic of his acting skill and rise to fame, the author even acknowledging that critics 'knock' Hudson's work 'by reflex'. Hudson by now seems resigned to this line of questioning but still challenges the easy assumptions that it is based on. He tells the reporter, 'When finally they put my name above the title I'd been building up to it for three, four years … and in the meantime I was studying 10 hours a day' (ibid.). His view of television seems as jaded as it had been five years earlier: 'You shoot so much per day you can't keep track. You shoot 10 or 12 pages of dialogue on a day where on film you shoot 3 maybe … . You become like a robot' (ibid.).

Following the demise of *McMillan & Wife*, Hudson appeared in several further made-for-TV movies and miniseries, including *Wheels* (1978), *The Martian Chronicles* (1980), *The Starmaker* (1981) and *The Devlin Connection* (1982). The latter spawned a TV series of the same name, made by Hudson's own production company. It was cancelled almost as soon as it was aired. While television work was rarely a satisfying experience for Hudson, it was working with Carol Burnett on her own TV show that led to his surprise triumph as a stage actor in a touring revival of a production of *I Do I Do* (1966) first with Burnett in the US and later in London's West End with Juliet Prowse.

In 1984, he returned to the genre that had secured his stardom thirty years earlier when he was cast as the 'millionaire horse trader' Daniel Reece in the phenomenally successfully television soap opera *Dynasty*. By this time he had aged noticeably. Although the role was standard soap-opera fare, Hudson's gaunt appearance, as well as the associated speculation surrounding his health, became a much bigger story than the part he was playing. By the time that his AIDS diagnosis was made public, a scene in which Daniel passionately kisses Krystle Carrington (Linda Evans) became a worldwide news story. Hudson featured in only nine episodes of *Dynasty* but this final kiss, performed by an actor who had gained such international success as a romantic lead, has become one of the defining moments of his career.

Hudson's last appearance on screen, in the wake of a media furore following the announcement that he had AIDS, was with his old friend and co-star Doris Day, in a specially filmed segment of her new show (made for the Christian Broadcasting Network and designed to relaunch her own television career) *Doris Day's Best Friends* in 1985. By the time that the show was broadcast Rock Hudson was already dead.

Postscript/post mortem

In the days leading up to and following Hudson's death, his AIDS diagnosis and details of his private life became global news, with thousands of articles iterating what was to become the orthodox 'story' of his life. This pivotal moment of personal tragedy was the point at which what Rock Hudson meant, as a public figure and also as a film star, was radically altered. As the first Hollywood star to 'succumb' to AIDS (in the hyperbolic turn of phrase common at that time), he went on to be portrayed as a star who 'lived a lie'. The narrative of deception took hold regardless of the fact that Hudson's homosexuality was an open secret in Hollywood; that the press had regularly colluded with Universal throughout his career to suppress this 'revelation'; and that rumours had consistently surfaced nonetheless. In large part this was because it mapped onto a wider contemporary atmosphere of panic and hysteria about AIDS that was directed at gay men. Simon Watney's astute analysis of the refiguring of Hudson in light of his diagnosis and death indicates the vitriolic and phobic nature of press coverage (in this case, the UK press) and the ways in which the disparity between his public persona and private life are marshalled to summon up a climate of homophobia: 'The central focus of Hudson's death concerns firstly a denunciation of "dishonesty", secondly a "betrayal" of male and female fans' fantasies, and thirdly the imputation of a guilty sense of responsibility for their illness to people with AIDS' (1987: 88).

In addition to the blanket news coverage of the story, several books were published in the months and years following Hudson's death to capitalise on the currency (and perceived sensationalism) of the story. As soon as Hudson had realised his grave condition (and no doubt because he was all too aware of the interest it would arouse), he had commissioned Sara Davidson to produce an authorised biography, *Rock Hudson: His Story*. Davidson was given full access to the actor's inner circle and the resulting book, written in haste given the limited time left to gain access to the star, was both extremely detailed and surprisingly honest, rendering all other attempts to uncover his private life redundant. In a rather unfortunately framed article from 1986 with Roger Ebert (which illustrates the commonplace ignorance about AIDS at the time), Davidson admitted:

Actually, I found out a lot more about Rock Hudson's sex life than I wanted to put in the book. I know what he liked, and how, and with whom, but I didn't think it was in good taste to go into all the graphic details.[16]

Davidson's book was published almost simultaneously with Jerry Oppenheimer and Jack Vitek's unauthorised *Idol: Rock Hudson, The True Story of an American Film Hero* and in an unedifying article Davidson was to dismiss her rival publication on the basis that she had secured the best sources and provided the strongest story.[17] These books were followed by an account from Hudson's ex-wife, Phyllis Gates, *My Husband Rock Hudson* published in 1987, another by an ex-lover, *Rock Hudson: Friend of Mine* (1990), Armistead Maupin's revelations that he had a sexual relationship with the star[18] and two books subsequent to the acrimonious court proceedings over the settlement of Hudson's estate: *The Trial of Rock Hudson* (1990) and *Between a Rock and a Hard Place: In Defence of Rock Hudson* (2010).

Within the context of this book, which is a consideration of Hudson's performances, the extent of this coverage is important because it becomes apparent from the style and nature of the stories told that 'acting' becomes a site for articulating over and over again the 'problem' of Hudson's sexuality and, consequently, it assumes a very particular significance during this period. At the start of Hudson's career, he was criticised for his 'lack' of acting ability. While he was a major Hollywood star his 'naturalness' on screen was dismissed as evidence that he was not really 'acting' at all, yet in this new revision of Hudson he is condemned for 'living a lie' and by inference (and also frequently explicitly) for being too convincing as a heterosexual heartthrob. This was a fairly radical reversal in terms of the perception of Hudson's persona and credentials as an actor. The skills that he was accused of lacking were now regarded as markers of deception and insincerity. I would argue that this provides clear evidence of how ideals of authenticity and truth, so bound up in masculine representation, are central to what Hudson symbolised as a star and what he was performing as an actor.

The first wave of the AIDS crisis and a climate of latent homophobia furnished a context in which Hudson and his performances were repositioned and politicised while a process of reappraisal and revisionism began to take place. This was to take several forms. Not long after Hudson's death, Richard Dyer noted that 'knowing that Rock was homosexual can alter the dynamics of looking … . This is not at all the same as suggesting that Rock's sexuality was thus expressed in his performance' (2001: 169). In making this case, in a thoughtful and reflective essay originally written in 1985, Dyer cautions against the kind of revisionism of Hudson that was to later emerge. In the early 1990s, Barbara Klinger argued in her book *Melodrama and Meaning* that the knowledge of his homosexuality inevitably inflected the way Hudson's performances were received. She suggested that his films are *now* understood by audiences through an ironicising lens that she regards as a camp reading position available to a wider, not exclusively gay audience. She terms this reading strategy 'mass camp' (1994: 132–57).

It is in this context of a rethinking of the meaning of Hudson, that the emergent Queer Theory adopted the actor as an object of study, enabling a discussion of AIDS and its positioning as the so-called 'gay plague' as well as the construction of heterosexuality and its ambivalences. For example, the queer film-maker John Greyson used alternating images of Hudson in *Ice Station Zebra*, his AIDS headlines together with pornographic material to illustrate the perverse and contradictory construction of gay sexuality in his film *Moscow Doesn't Believe in Queers* (1986). Richard Meyer's essay 'Rock Hudson's Body' offers a comparative reading of how Hudson was represented in his hey-day and how he was to be represented as a gay man with AIDS. The essay is careful to foreground the impossibility of gay representation in mid-1950s Hollywood cinema but suggests, nonetheless, that Hudson's homosexuality was 'registered in his star image' (1991: 279). While it is hard to reconcile this conclusion with the evidence, it has nonetheless become an influential essay and played a part in a larger project that can be described as an *archaeology* of Hudson's homosexual representations in cinema, the epitome of which (for better or worse) being provided by Mark Rappaport's film *Rock Hudson's Home Movies* (1992). Rappaport's film is very much a product of its historical/cultural moment and production context. The low production values and DIY aesthetic are in keeping with the initial phase of what would become known as New Queer Cinema. Through the use of multiple clips of Hudson in films from across his career, as well as a process of highly selective editing, a collage of fragments of film is built up, overlaid by the voice of a narrator (Eric Farr), who appears to be recounting reminiscences from the actor's (fictional) diary. In an essay in *Film Quarterly*, the director justified his methods and approach thus:

In my format, you bring the source to the spectator. Even if the scene is out of context, the authenticity of what is presented, what is seen and heard, is undeniable. You are not subject to the additional, and unreliable, barrier of a secondary source's impression of whatever it was they think they saw. (Rappaport 1996: 22)

Despite Rappaport's protestations, the resulting film is inherently subjective and presented to an audience expressly as the result of a director's vision/revision (or perhaps more accurately 'version') of

Hudson. The 'repurposing' of found footage is designed to make strategic use of Hudson as a figure in order to expose a homosexuality that is disavowed in wider culture. This political ambition is to be realised through deconstruction and through the cumulative power of momentary fragments that seem to speak a 'truth' that is denied. In practice the film's ambition to expose what is suppressed is undermined by its didacticism. The nuance, subtlety and ambiguity in many of the films that *Rock Hudson's Home Movies* is aiming to repurpose tend to get lost in the process. Ultimately (even though it's largely unintentional), the merit of Rappaport's film is that it offers its audience a kaleidoscope of fascinating glimpses and fragments of performances that were all too often dismissed or derided. It, in fact, enables us to see in microcosm the technical virtuosity of some of these performances and, while it only partially achieves its stated objective, the film does succeed in presenting Hudson as an accomplished screen actor. This finally illustrates, for me at least, the enduring enigma and appeal of this most underestimated of Hollywood's leading men.

NOTES

1 The apprenticeship, 1948–54

1 See *E! True Hollywood Story: Rock Hudson* (TV 1999).

2 A much more detailed and entertaining, if rather lurid, account of the story and working practices of Henry Willson and his relationship with Hudson and his other clients can be found in Robert Hofler's *The Man Who Invented Rock Hudson: The Pretty Boys and the Dirty Deals of Henry Willson* (2005).

3 See Anthony Slide's *Inside the Hollywood Fan Magazine: A History of Star Makers, Fabricators and Gossip Mongers* (2010).

4 Cynthia Baron's essay, 'Crafting Film Performances: Acting in the Hollywood Studio Era' (2004) features an extensive discussion of the acting manuals prevalent at the time and, in particular, the work of Lillian Burns, Sophie Rosenstein and Lillian Albertson. The essay considers the ways in which these source texts informed the development of a film performance and strategy that actors could deploy to manage the production-line processes of the studio system.

5 For a concise explanation and discussion of method acting in Hollywood cinema, see Virginia Wright Wexman's 'Masculinity in Crisis: Method Acting in Hollywood' (2004).

6 See James Gilbert's *Men in the Middle: Searching for Masculinity in the 1950s* (2005). Through a close analysis of a range of materials and literature, Gilbert challenges the received wisdom around fixed gender roles in the period.

7 See Tino Balio's *Grand Design: Hollywood as a Modern Business Enterprise, 1930–1939* (1995) and also 'Selling Stars: The Economic Imperative' (2012) for a detailed and useful discussion of the structure of the acting profession in Hollywood.

2 The tall, dark and handsome star

1 Hunter was one of the first producers to use records as a marketing tool to 'pre-sell' a film, with the Debbie Reynolds vehicle *Tammy* in 1957. See Natt Freedland's article in *Billboard*, 9 September 1972.

2 Sirk's status as a subversive 'Brechtian' auteur is not without challenge and an interesting and thoroughgoing critique of the orthodoxy of this and other positions within film studies is offered by Robert B. Ray in *How a Film Theory Got Lost: And Other Mysteries in Cultural Studies* (2001).

3 See Christine Gledhill's *Home Is Where the Heart Is* (1987), which not only features Gledhill's forensic survey of debate around melodrama but also gathers together the work of Thomas Elsaesser (including 'Tales of Sound and Fury: Observations on the Family Melodrama') and Laura Mulvey's 'Notes on Sirk and Melodrama'. See also the essays 'Distanciation and Douglas Sirk' (1971) and 'Towards an Analysis of the Sirkian System' (1972) by Paul Willemen, Fred Camper's 'The Films of Douglas Sirk' (1971) in *Screen*, as well as Rainer Werner Fassbinder's 'Six Films by Douglas Sirk' (1975) in *New Left Review*. Books include Jackie Byars's *All That Hollywood Allows: Re-reading Gender in 1950s Melodrama* (1991), Barbara Klinger's *Melodrama and Meaning* (1994), as well as Mercer and Shingler's *Melodrama: Genre Style Sensibility* (2004). For a concise summary, see my contribution on melodrama to the *Schirmer Encyclopedia of Film* (2005).

4 The sections where Sirk mentions Hudson's homosexuality do not appear in the original 1971 edition of *Sirk on Sirk*, only being included in the revised edition of 1997, published after Hudson's death.

5 See James Naremore's 'The Performance Frame' in *Star Texts: Image and Performance in Film and Television* (1991).

6 Nine films if *Never Say Goodbye* is included as this bears his unmistakable imprimatur if not his name as director. Sirk was involved in both the early and final stages of the production.

7 While Jean Luc Godard had reviewed Sirk's *A Time to Love and a Time to Die* in 1959, the key moment in the critical reappraisal began with the publication of an interview with the director: Jean-Louis Noames and Serge Daney, 'Entretien avec Douglas Sirk' in 1967.

8 See an interview with Carole Langer in 1996 from a series that was filmed (though never broadcast). Available at http://www.youtube.com/watch?v=Zigbtfanhs4.

9 See Bernard F. Dick's (1997: 148) account of the production of the film in *City of Dreams: The Making and Remaking of Universal Pictures*.

10 See Maureen Turim's 'Designing Women: The Emergence of the New Sweet Heart Line' (1990) and also Stella Bruzzi's analysis of the use of costume in the film in 'It Will Be a Magnificent Obsession' (2011).

11 Several subsequent radio adaptations were produced of this especially popular story with Claudette Colbert and Myrna Loy in the starring role. The film was also adapted for television in 1949 with Dunne reprising her role.

12 The key proponent of which was Edith Skinner, the voice coach and author of *Speaking with Distinction* (1942).

13 Sirk's cinematographer Russell Metty is quoted as saying that Hudson had the 'perfect face for a close up' because unlike most actors he had no 'weak side' in an article in the *Deseret News and Telegram* in 1954.

14 By May 1954 his billing was such that he featured in a photo spread in *Life* magazine called 'The Stronger Sex Makes Strong Box Office' about the new generation of leading men, appearing alongside Kirk Douglas, Burt Lancaster and William Holden. Hudson is presented as 'youthful' in a lively shot on a rope ladder with Tony Curtis and a young Robert Wagner. By September of the same year and following the success of *Magnificent Obsession*, *Life* magazine describes the

film as a 'turning point' in his career in a feature on Hudson's rise to fame.

15 In fact, there was only an eight-year age difference between Wyman (born in 1917) and Hudson (born in 1925). While there is no explicit mention of age in the film, it is implicit throughout that the age gap is wider than this.

16 The second being the clambake scene at Mick (Charles Drake) and Alida's (Virginia Grey) home where Ron dances and sings.

17 See Mark Jancovich's '"Charlton Heston Is an Axiom": Spectacle and Performance in the Development of the Blockbuster' (2004).

18 See James Naremore's discussion of the influence of Delsarte on American acting and the silent cinema acting style in *Acting in the Cinema* (1988: 34–67). See also Lael Woodbury, 'The Externalization of Emotion' (1960) and E. T. Kirby, 'The Delsarte Method: 3 Frontiers of Actor Training' (1972).

19 See Paul Willemen, 'Notes on the Sirkian System', *Screen* vol. 12 no. 2 (1971) and 'Towards an Analysis of the Sirkian System', *Screen* vol. 13 no. 4 (1972).

20 Elia Kazan, one of the founders of the Actors Studio, home of the 'method', interestingly said in his autobiography that he saw no technique in Dean's acting at all (1988: 538).

21 See David Dalton's chapter on the making of *Giant* in *James Dean: The Mutant King* (1983: 267).

22 Indeed, an article in *Collier's Weekly* in 1956 entitled 'School for Stars' informs us that several Hollywood luminaries, including Rock Hudson, had visited the Actors Studio to study and observe.

23 The film is sometimes incorrectly attributed to Douglas Sirk. However, Sirk was to tell Jon Halliday that his involvement was in preproduction (the casting of the German actress Cornell Borchers) and in completing the film, which was being made at the same time as *Written on the Wind* (1997: 121).

3 'Adult' content and the mature actor

1 The same article positioned Hudson alongside, among others, Marlon Brando, described as 'Dramatic Actor', Kim Novak, 'Box Office Blonde', William Wyler, 'Prize Director' and Elizabeth Taylor, 'Dramatic Actress'.

2 See Babbington and Evans (1989), Hirsch (2010), Robertson Wojcik (2010), Glitre (2006), Mortimer (2010) and Jeffers McDonald (2007).

3 Although Freud famously regarded America as a 'mistake' he was enthusiastically received in 1909 and his ideas were embraced more quickly and initially much more enthusiastically in the US than in Europe. See Freud's *An Autobiographical Study* (1925) and Betty Friedan's critical analysis of Freud's contribution to American cultural discourse in *The Feminine Mystique* (1963).

4 See James Gilbert's detailed summary of the context for and impact of the release of the first Kinsey report in *Men in the Middle* (2005: 81–106).

5 For James Gilbert, *The Feminine Mystique* marks, socially and culturally, the end of the period we generically describe as the 1950s, as it indicates the point at which Friedan calls for concrete change to American values through changing the condition of women (2005: 217–19).

6 See Barbara Klinger's commentary in *Melodrama and Meaning* (1994: 112–16).

7 I am indebted to the website *The Rock Hudson Project* and, in particular, its archive of press cuttings, including a collection of Hudson's work in commercials.

8 This duality was disrupted for a period during Hudson's marriage to Phyllis Gates from 1955 to 1958, reputedly arranged by Henry Willson to suppress rumours about his homosexuality.

9 Gordon had been blacklisted and was not able to work in Hollywood again until the late 1950s.

10 See Bill Osgerby's essay 'The Bachelor Pad as Cultural Icon: Masculinity, Consumption and Interior Design in American Men's Magazines, 1930–65' (2005). See also Mark Jancovich's 'The Politics of *Playboy*: Lifestyle, Sexuality and Non-conformity in American Cold War Culture'

(2006); and Steven Cohan, 'Cary Grant in the Fifties: Indiscretions of the Bachelor's Masquerade' (1992).

11 See Richard Barrios's *Screened Out: Playing Gay in Hollywood from Edison to Stonewall* (2005) and Wheeler Winston Dixon's *Straight: Constructions of Heterosexuality in the Cinema* (2003). Vito Russo's brief comments about *A Very Special Favor* in *The Celluloid Closet* are an interesting indicator of the ways in which films of this sort can be read with a specific intention. Russo argues that Chadwick is 'basically insecure, he really does not do well with women, and the constant strain of the pretence drives him crazy' (1987: 114), which seems a misunderstanding of the film's narrative, to say the least.

12 For a discussion of the production context for Meyer's film, see Jon Lewis, *Hollywood vs Hard Core: How the Struggle over Censorship Created the Modern Film Industry* (2002: 175–6).

13 What might seem even more unlikely is that the script was written by *Star Trek* creator Gene Roddenberry and the film's title track performed by the cleancut Osmonds.

14 The quote here is used in Heather Addison's excellent essay, ' "Must the Players Keep Young?" Early Hollywood's Cult of Youth' (2006), about the social and cultural emergence of this youth-oriented bias in early Hollywood cinema.

15 See Scott Eyman, *Five American Cinematographers: Interviews with Karl Struss, Joseph Ruttenberg, James Wong Howe, Linwood Dunn, and William H. Clothier* (1987). Wong Howe discusses working with Frankenheimer and the conflict between his own desire to innovate and the frenetic working practices of the director.

16 See http://www.rogerebert.com/balder-and-dash/rock-hudsons-secret.

17 See http://articles.philly.com/1986-06-29/entertainment/26042762_1_rock-hudson-jack-vitek-sara-davidson.

18 See Patrick Gale, *Armistead Maupin* (1999).

BIBLIOGRAPHY

Addison, H., *Hollywood and the Rise of Physical Culture* (London: Routledge, 2003).

Addison, H., '"Must the Players Keep Young?" Early Hollywood's Cult of Youth', *Cinema Journal* vol. 45 no. 4 (2006), pp. 3–25.

Affron, C., 'Performing Performing: Irony and Affect', *Cinema Journal* vol. 20 no. 1 (1980), pp. 42–52.

Albertson, L., *Motion Picture Acting* (New York: Funk and Wagnalls Company, 1947).

Alpert, H., 'The Movies: It's Dean, Dean, Dean', *Saturday Review*, 13 October 1956, pp. 28–9.

Alpert, H., 'The Movies: A Second Farewell', *Saturday Review*, 1 February 1958, p. 27.

Altman, R., 'Reusable Packaging: Generic Products and the Recycling Process', in N. Browne (ed.), *Refiguring American Film Genres: History and Theory* (Berkeley: University of California Press, 1998).

Amossy, R., 'Autobiographies of Movie Stars: Presentation of Self and Its Strategies', *Poetics Today* vol. 7 no. 4 (1986), pp. 673–703.

Anon., 'The Stronger Sex Makes Strong Box Office', *Life Magazine*, May 1954, pp. 93–6.

Anon., 'Rock Hudson Has Perfect Face for Close-up', *Deseret News and Telegram*, 12 July 1954, p. 11.

Anon., 'Two Careers Take a Turn', *Life Magazine*, September 1954, pp. 51–6.

Anon., 'Muscles Make Hollywood Stars', *Tomorrow's Man*, February 1956, pp. 4–6.

Anon., 'School for Stars', *Collier's Weekly*, 16 March 1956, pp. 26–31.

Anon., '20 Year Old's Ideal: Perry Como, Their Choice, Enacts Perfect Spouse', *Life Magazine*, December 1956, pp.143–5.

Anon., 'The Real Rock Hudson', *Fans' Star Library*, October 1958.

Anon., 'People at the Top of Entertainment's World', *Life Magazine*, December 1958, pp. 159–68.

Armstrong, S. B., *John Frankenheimer: Interviews, Essays and Profiles* (Plymouth: Scarecrow Press, 2013).

Babbington, B. and Evans, P. W., *Affairs to Remember: The Hollywood Comedy of the Sexes* (Manchester: Manchester University Press, 1989).

Balio, T., *Grand Design: Hollywood as a Modern Business Enterprise, 1930–1939* (Berkeley: University of California Press, 1995).

Balio, T., 'Selling Stars: The Economic Imperative', in S. Neale (ed.), *The Classical Hollywood Reader* (London: Routledge, 2012).

Baron, C., 'Crafting Film Performances: Acting in the Hollywood Studio Era', in P. Wojcik (ed.), *Movie Acting: The Film Reader* (London: Routledge, 2004).

Baron, C. and Carnicke, S., *Reframing Screen Performance* (Ann Arbor: University of Michigan Press, 2008).

Barrios, R., *Screened Out: Playing Gay in Hollywood from Edison to Stonewall* (London: Routledge, 2005).

Barton Palmer, R., 'Charlton Heston and Gregory Peck: Organization Men', in R. Barton Palmer (ed.), *Larger than Life: Movie Stars of the 1950s* (Piscataway, NJ: Rutgers University Press, 2010).

Basinger, J., *A Woman's View: How Hollywood Spoke to Women 1930–60* (London: Chatto & Windus, 1993).

Basinger, J., *Anthony Mann* (Middletown, CT: Wesleyan University Press, 2007).

Bell-Metereau, R., 'Stealth, Sexuality, and Cult Status in *The Manchurian Candidate* and *Seconds*', in R. Barton Palmer and M. Pommerance (eds), *A Little Solitaire: John Frankenheimer and American Film* (Piscataway, NJ: Rutgers University Press, 2011).

Black, P., *The Beauty Insider: Gender, Culture, Pleasure* (London: Routledge, 2004).

Bret, D., *Rock Hudson* (London: Robson Books, 2005).

Breward, C., 'Manliness, Modernity and the Shaping of Male Clothing', in J. Entwistle and E. Wilson (eds), *Body Dressing* (Oxford: Berg, 2001).

Brooks, P., *The Melodramatic Imagination: Balzac, Henry James, Melodrama and the Mode of Excess* (New Haven, CT: Yale University Press, 1976).

Browne, N. (ed.), *Refiguring American Film Genres: History and Theory* (Berkeley: University of California Press, 1998).

Bruzzi, S., 'It Will Be a Magnificent Obsession', in A. Munich (ed.), *Fashion in Film* (Bloomington: Indiana University Press, 2011).

Byars, J., *All That Hollywood Allows: Re-reading Gender in 1950s Melodrama* (London: Routledge, 1991).

Campbell, J., *The Hero with a Thousand Faces* (New York: Pantheon, 1949).

Casper, D., *Hollywood Film 1963–1976: Years of Revolution and Reaction* (London: Wiley-Blackwell, 2011).

Chopra Grant, M., *Hollywood Genres and Postwar America: Masculinity, Family and Nation in Popular Movies and Film Noir* (London: I. B. Tauris, 2006).

Clark, D., *Negotiating Hollywood: The Cultural Politics of Actors' Labour* (Minneapolis: University of Minnesota Press, 1995).

Clifton Moore, R., 'Pacifism in Film: Exclusion and Containment as Hegemonic Processes', in P. Loukides and L. Fuller (eds), *Beyond the Stars: Studies in American Popular Film* (Bowling Green, OH: Bowling Green State University Popular Press, 1996).

Cohan, S., 'Cary Grant in the Fifties: Indiscretions of the Bachelor's Masquerade', *Screen* vol. 33 no. 4 (1992), pp. 394–412.

Cohan, S., *Masked Men: Masculinity and the Movies in the Fifties* (Bloomington: Indiana University Press, 1997).

Cook, P., 'Melodrama and the Women's Picture', in M. Landy (ed.), *Imitations of Life: A Reader on Film and Television Melodrama* (Detroit, MI: Wayne State University Press, 1991).

Corkin, S., 'Cowboys and Free Markets: Post-World War II Westerns and U.S. Hegemony', *Cinema Journal* vol. 39 no. 3 (2000), pp. 66–91.

Crowther, B., 'Review of *The Lost Weekend*', in *New York Times Film Reviews* vol. 3: 1939–1948 (1945), p. 2128.

Crowther, B., 'The Screen: Pillow Talk', *New York Times*, 7 October 1959.

Dalton, D., *James Dean: Mutant King* (New York: St Martin's Press, 1983).

Davidson, J. and Hudson, R., *Rock Hudson: His Story* (London: Weidenfeld & Nicholson, 1986).

Davis, R. L., *Just Making Movies: Company Directors on the Studio System* (Jackson: University of Mississippi Press, 2005).

DeCordova, R., *Picture Personalities: The Emergence of the Star System in Hollywood* (Chicago: University of Illinois Press, 1990).

Dick, B. F., *City of Dreams: The Making and Remaking of Universal Pictures* (Lexington: University of Kentucky Press, 1997).

Dixon, S., 'Ambiguous Ecologies: Stardom's Domestic Mise-en-scène', *Cinema Journal* vol. 42 no. 2 (Winter 2003), pp. 81–100.

Dixon, Wheeler W., *Straight: Constructions of Heterosexuality in the Cinema* (Albany: State University of New York Press, 2003).

Dunning, J., *On the Air: The Encyclopedia of Old-Time Radio* (New York: Oxford University Press, 1998).

Dyer, R., *Stars* (London: BFI, 1999).

Dyer, R., *The Culture of Queers* (London: Routledge, 2001).

Elsaesser, T., 'Tales of Sound and Fury: Observations on the Family Melodrama', in C. Gledhill (ed.), *Home Is Where the Heart Is: Studies in Melodrama and the Woman's Film* (London: BFI, 1987).

Evans, P. W., 'From Maria Montez to Jasmine: Hollywood's Oriental Odalisques', in I. Santaolalla (ed.), *New Exoticisms: Changing Patterns in the Construction of Otherness* (Amsterdam: Editions Rodopi B.V., 2000).

Eyman, S., *Five American Cinematographers: Interviews with Karl Struss, Joseph Ruttenberg, James Wong Howe, Linwood Dunn, and William H. Clothier* (Lanham, MD: Scarecrow Press, 1987).

Farber, S., '*Seconds* by John Frankenheimer', *Film Quarterly* (Winter 1966–7), pp. 25–8.

Freedland, D., 'Ross Hunter Seeks Pre-sell Ideas for *Lost Horizon* Film Music', *Billboard*, September 1972, p. 4.

Friedan, B., *The Feminine Mystique* (New York: W. W. Norton and Company, 1963).

Gale, P., *Armistead Maupin* (Bath: Absolute Press, 1999).

Gilbert, J., *Men in the Middle: Searching for Masculinity in the 1950s* (Chicago, IL: University of Chicago Press, 2005).

Giles, J., 'Class, Gender and Domestic Consumption in Britain 1920–1950', in E. Casey and L. Martin (eds), *Gender and Consumption: Domestic Cultures and the Commercialisation of Everyday Life* (Aldershot: Ashgate, 2007).

Gledhill, C. (ed.), *Home Is Where the Heart Is: Studies in Melodrama and the Woman's Film* (London: BFI, 1987).

Gledhill, C. (ed.), *Stardom: Industry of Desire* (London: Routledge, 1991).

Gledhill, C. and Williams, L. (eds), *Reinventing Film Studies* (London: Hodder Arnold, 2000).

Glitre, K., *Hollywood Romantic Comedy: States of the Union 1934–65* (Manchester: Manchester University Press, 2006).

Gurley Brown, H., *Sex and the Single Girl: The Unmarried Woman's Guide to Men, Careers, the Apartment, Diet, Fashion, Money and Men* (New York: Bernard Geis Associates, 1960).

Halliday, J., *Sirk on Sirk: Conversations with Jon Halliday* (London: Secker & Warburg, 1972).

Halliday, J., *Sirk on Sirk: Conversations with Jon Halliday*, rev. edn (London: Faber and Faber, 1997).

Higson, A., 'Film Acting and Independent Cinema', in P. Wojcik (ed.), *Movie Acting: The Film Reader* (London: Routledge, 2004).

Hirsch, F. , 'Doris Day and Rock Hudson: The Girl Next Door and the Brawny He-Man', in R. Barton Palmer (ed.), *Larger than Life: Movie Stars of the 1950s* (Piscataway, NJ: Rutgers University Press, 2010).

Hofler, R., *The Man Who Invented Rock Hudson: The Pretty Boys and Dirty Deals of Henry Willson* (New York: Carroll & Graf, 2005).

Hollander, A., *Sex and Suits* (New York: Alfred A. Knopf, 1994).

Howe, H., 'Returning to Hollywood', *Photoplay Magazine*, May 1925, p. 30.

Hudson, R., 'Public Reaction Greater on TV, Says Rock Hudson', *Lawrence Daily Journal-World*, 17 July 1972, p. 23.

Jancovich, M., ' "Charlton Heston Is an Axiom": Spectacle and Performance in the Development of the Blockbuster', in A. Willis (ed.), *Film Stars: Hollywood and Beyond* (Manchester: Manchester University Press, 2004).

Jancovich, M., 'The Politics of *Playboy*: Lifestyle, Sexuality and Non-conformity in American Cold War Culture', in D. Bell and J. Hollows (eds), *Historicizing Lifestyle: Mediating Taste, Consumption and Identity from the 1900s to 1970s* (Aldershot: Ashgate, 2006).

Jeffers McDonald, T., 'Very Little Wrist Movement: Rock Hudson Acts Out Sexual Heterodoxy', *Canadian Journal of Communication* vol. 31 (2006), pp. 843–58.

Jeffers McDonald, T., *Romantic Comedy: Boy Meets Girl Meets Genre* (London: Columbia University Press, 2007).

Jeffers McDonald, T., *Doris Day Confidential: Hollywood, Sex and Stardom* (London: I. B. Tauris, 2013).

Kalfatovic, M., 'Rock Hudson', in R. P. Browne and P. Browne (eds), *The Guide to United States Popular Culture* (Madison: University of Wisconsin Press, 2001).

Kazan, E., *Elia Kazan: A Life* (New York: Da Capo Press, Inc., 1988).

Kemper, T., *Hidden Talent: The Emergence of Hollywood Agents* (Berkeley: University of California Press, 2010).

Kimmel, M., *Manhood in America: A Cultural History* (New York: Free Press, 1996).

Kinsey, A., Pomeroy, W. and Martin, C., *Sexual Behaviour in the Human Male* (Philadelphia, PA: W. B. Saunders and Company, 1948).

Kirby, E. T., 'The Delsarte Method: 3 Frontiers of Actor Training', *Drama Review: TDR* vol. 16 no. 1 (1972), pp. 55–69.

Klinger, B., *Melodrama and Meaning: History, Culture and the Films of Douglas Sirk* (Bloomington: Indiana University Press, 1994).

Knight, A., 'Stereotypes, and Acting in Films', *College English* vol. 15 no. 1 (1953), pp. 1–7.

Knox, A., 'Acting and Behaving', *Hollywood Quarterly* vol. 1 no. 3 (1946), pp. 260–9.

Levy, E., *John Wayne: Prophet of the American Way of Life* (Lanham, MD: Scarecrow Press, 1998).

Lewis, J., *Hollywood vs Hard Core: How the Struggle over Censorship Created the Modern Film Industry* (New York: New York University Press, 2002).

Mackinnon, K., *Uneasy Pleasures: The Male as Erotic Object* (London: Cygnus Arts, 1997).

Maltby, R., *Hollywood Cinema* (London: Wiley-Blackwell, 1997).

Mason-Brown, J., *Dramatis Personae* (New York: Viking Press, 1963).

McCracken, J., *Taste and the Household: The Domestic Aesthetic and Moral Reasoning* (Albany: State University of New York Press, 2001).

Mercer, J., 'Melodrama', in B. K. Grant (ed.), *Schirmer Encyclopedia of Film* (Detroit, MI: Thomson Gale, 2005).

Mercer, J. and Shingler, S., *Melodrama: Genre, Style, Sensibility* (New York: Columbia University Press, 2004).

Meyer, R., 'Rock Hudson's Body', in D. Fuss (ed.), *Inside/Out: Lesbian Theories/Gay Theories* (New York: Routledge, 1991).

Morin, E., *The Stars: An Account of the Star System in Motion Pictures* (New York: Grove Press, 1961).

Morris, G. (ed.), *Action! Interviews with Directors from Classical Hollywood to Contemporary Iran* (London: Anthem Press, 2009).

Mortimer, C., *Romantic Comedy* (London: Routledge, 2010).

Moss, M. A., *Giant: George Stevens, a Life on Film* (Madison: University of Wisconsin Press, 2004).

Moss, M. A., *Raoul Walsh: The True Adventures of Hollywood's Legendary Director* (Lexington: University of Kentucky Press, 2011).

Mourlet, M., 'In Defence of Violence', in C. Gledhill (ed.), *Stardom: Industry of Desire* (London: Routledge, 1991).

Mulvey, L., 'Notes on Sirk and Melodrama', in C. Gledhill (ed.), *Home Is Where the Heart Is: Studies in Melodrama and the Woman's Film* (London: BFI, 1987).

Naremore, J., *Acting in the Cinema* (Berkeley: University of California Press, 1988).

Naremore, J., 'The Performance Frame', in J. G. Butler (ed.), *Star Texts: Image and Performance in Film and Television* (Detroit, MI: Wayne State University Press, 1991).

Neupert, R., *A History of the French New Wave Cinema* (Madison: University of Wisconsin Press, 2007).

Neve, B., *Elia Kazan: The Cinema of an American Outsider* (London: I. B. Tauris, 2009).

Nichols, B. (ed.), *Movies and Methods vol. I* (Berkeley: University of California Press, 1976).

Noames, J. L. and Daney, S., 'Entretien avec Douglas Sirk', *Cahiers du cinéma* no. 189 (1967), pp. 19–25, 67.

Nussbaum, M., 'The "Adult Western" as an American Art Form', *Folklore* vol. 70 no. 3 (1959), pp. 460–7.

Oppenheimer, J. and Vitek, J., *Idol: Rock Hudson, The True Story of an American Film Hero* (New York: Villard Books, 1986).

Osgerby, B., 'The Bachelor Pad as Cultural Icon: Masculinity, Consumption and Interior Design in American Men's Magazines, 1930–65', *Journal of Design History* vol. 18 no. 1, *Publishing the Modern Home: Magazines and the Domestic Interior 1870–1965* (Spring 2005), pp. 99–113.

Parker, J., 'Rock Hudson: Did He Become a Star before He Became an Actor?', *Tuscaloosa News*, 2 July 1976, p. 2.

Parker, J., *The Trial of Rock Hudson* (London: Sidgwick & Jackson, 1990).

Pudovkin, V. I., *Film Technique and Film Acting* (London: Read Books, 1953).

Quart, L. and Auster, A., *American Film and Society since 1945* (London: Macmillan, 1984).

Rappaport, M., 'Mark Rappaport's Notes on "Rock Hudson's Home Movies"', *Film Quarterly* vol. 49 no. 4 (1996), pp. 16–22.

Ray, R. B., *How a Film Theory Got Lost and Other Mysteries in Cultural Studies* (Bloomington: Indiana University Press, 2001).

Richards, J., *Swordsmen of the Screen: From Douglas Fairbanks to Michael York* (London: Routledge and Kegan Paul, 1977).

Riesman, D., Glazer, N. and Denney, R., *The Lonely Crowd: A Study of the Changing American Character* (New Haven, CT: Yale University Press, 1950).

Robertson Wojcik, P., *The Apartment Plot: Urban Living in American Film and Popular Culture, 1945 to 1975* (Durham, NC: Duke University Press, 2010).

Rosenstein, S., Haydon, L. A. and Sparrow, W., *Modern Acting: A Manual* (New York: Samuel French, 1936).

Russo, V., *The Celluloid Closet: Homosexuality in the Movies* (New York: Harper & Row, 1987).

Sagolla, L. J., *The Girl Who Fell Down: A Biography of Joan McCracken* (Lebanon, TN: University of New England Press, 2003).

Schlesinger, A. M., 'The Crisis of American Masculinity', *The Politics of Hope and the Bitter Heritage: American Liberalism in the 1960s* (Princeton, NJ: Princeton University Press, 2008).

Shingler, M., *Star Studies: A Critical Guide* (London: BFI/Palgrave Macmillan, 2012).

Slide, A., *Inside the Hollywood Fan Magazine: A History of Star-makers, Fabricators and Gossip Mongers* (Jackson: University of Mississippi Press, 2010).

Slocom, J. D., 'Cinema and the Civilizing Process: Rethinking Violence in the World War II Combat Film', *Cinema Journal* vol. 44 no. 3 (2005), pp. 35–63.

Smyth, J. E., *Edna Ferber's Hollywood: American Fictions of Gender, Race and History* (Austin: University of Texas Press, 2010).

Sobchak, V., *Screening Space: The American Science Fiction Film* (New Brunswick, NJ: Rutgers University Press, 2001).

Spoto, D., *Marilyn Monroe: The Biography* (New York: Copper Square Press, 1993).

Springer, C., *James Dean Transfigured: The Many Faces of Rebel Iconography* (Austin: University of Texas Press, 2007).

Staiger, J., *Interpreting Films: Studies in the Historical Reception of American Cinema* (Princeton, NJ: Princeton University Press, 1992).

Sterritt, D., 'Murdered Souls, Conspiratorial Cabals: Frankenheimer's Paranoia Films', in R. Barton Palmer and M. Pommerance (eds), *A Little Solitaire: John Frankenheimer and American Film* (Piscataway, NJ: Rutgers University Press, 2011).

Turim, M., 'Designing Women: The Emergence of the New Sweet Heart Line', in J. Gaines and C. Herzog (eds), *Fabrications: Costume and the Female Body* (London: Routledge, 1990).

Walker, A., *The Celluloid Sacrifice: Aspects of Sex in the Movies* (London: Michael Joseph, 1966).

Watney, S., *Policing Desire: Pornography, AIDS and the Media* (London: Comedia, 1987).

Willemen, P., 'Distanciation and Douglas Sirk', *Screen* vol. 12 no. 2 (1971), pp. 63–7.

Wilson, S., *The Man in the Gray Flannel Suit* (New York: Da Capo Press, 1955).

Winston Dixon, W., *Straight: Constructions of Heterosexuality in the Cinema* (Albany: State University of New York Press, 2003).

Woodbury, L. J., 'The Externalization of Emotion', *Educational Theatre Journal* vol. 12 no. 3 (1960), pp. 177–83.

Wright Mills, C., *White Collar: The American Middle Classes* (New York: Oxford University Press, 1951).

Wright Wexman, V., 'Masculinity in Crisis: Method Acting in Hollywood', in P. Wojcik (ed.), *Movie Acting: The Film Reader* (London: Routledge, 2004).

Zeitlin, D., 'Seen Any Good Titles Lately?', *Life Magazine*, February 1964, pp. 103–4.

FILMOGRAPHY

Feature films

FIGHTER SQUADRON (uncredited) (Raoul Walsh, USA, 1948), Second
   Lieutenant
UNDERTOW (as Roc Hudson) (William Castle, USA, 1948), Detective
ONE WAY STREET (uncredited) (Hugo Fregonese, USA, 1950), Truck
   driver
I WAS A SHOPLIFTER (Charles Lamont, USA, 1950), Store detective
PEGGY (Frederick De Cordova, USA, 1950), Johnny Mitchell
WINCHESTER '73 (Anthony Mann, USA, 1950), Young Bull
THE DESERT HAWK (Frederick De Cordova, USA, 1950), Captain
   Ras
SHAKEDOWN (Joseph Pevney, USA, 1950), Ted, the nightclub doorman
TOMAHAWK (George Sherman, USA, 1951), Burt Hanna
JET MEN OF THE AIR 'AIR CADET' (original title) (Joseph Pevney,
   USA, 1951), Upper classman
THE FAT MAN (William Castle, USA, 1951), Roy Clark
LIGHTS OUT 'BRIGHT VICTORY' (original title) (Mark Robson, USA,
   1951), Dudek
IRON MAN (Joseph Pevney, USA, 1951), O'Keefe
BEND OF THE RIVER (Anthony Mann, USA, 1952), Trey Wilson
HERE COME THE NELSONS (Frederick De Cordova, USA, 1952),
   Charlie Jones

SCARLET ANGEL (Sidney Salkow, USA, 1952), Frank Truscott

HAS ANYBODY SEEN MY GAL? (Douglas Sirk, USA, 1952), Dan Stebbins

HORIZONS WEST (Budd Boetticher, USA, 1952), Neil Hammond

THE LAWLESS BREED (Raoul Walsh, USA, 1953), John Wesley Hardin

SEMINOLE (Budd Boetticher, USA, 1953), Lance Caldwell

BACK TO GOD'S COUNTRY (Joseph Pevney, USA, 1953), Peter Keith

GUN FURY (Raoul Walsh, USA, 1953), Ben Warren

THE GOLDEN BLADE (Nathan Juran, USA, 1953), Harun

SEA DEVILS (Raoul Walsh, USA, 1953), Gilliatt

TAZA, SON OF COCHISE (Douglas Sirk, USA, 1954), Taza

MAGNIFICENT OBSESSION (Douglas Sirk, USA, 1954), Bob Merrick

BENGAL RIFLES 'BENGAL BRIGADE' (original title) (Laslo Benedek, USA, 1954), Captain Jeffrey Claybourne

CAPTAIN LIGHTFOOT (Douglas Sirk, USA, 1955), Michael Martin

ONE DESIRE (Jerry Hopper, USA, 1955), Clint Saunders

ALL THAT HEAVEN ALLOWS (Douglas Sirk, USA, 1955), Ron Kirby

NEVER SAY GOODBYE (Jerry Hopper, USA, 1956), Dr. Michael Parker

GIANT (George Stevens, USA, 1956), Bick Benedict

WRITTEN ON THE WIND (Douglas Sirk, USA, 1956), Mitch Wayne

BATTLE HYMN (Douglas Sirk, USA, 1957), Colonel Dean Hess

SOMETHING OF VALUE (Richard Brooks, USA, 1957), Peter

THE TARNISHED ANGELS (Douglas Sirk, USA, 1957), Burke Devlin

A FAREWELL TO ARMS (Charles Vidor, USA, 1957), Lt Frederick Henry

TWILIGHT FOR THE GODS (Joseph Pevney, USA, 1958), Captain David Bell

THIS EARTH IS MINE (Henry King, USA, 1959), John Rambeau

PILLOW TALK (Michael Gordon, USA, 1959), Brad Allen

THE LAST SUNSET (Robert Aldrich, USA, 1961), Dana Stribling

COME SEPTEMBER (Robert Mulligan, USA, 1961), Robert L. Talbot

LOVER COME BACK (Delbert Mann, USA, 1961), Jerry Webster

THE SPIRAL ROAD (Robert Mulligan, USA, 1962), Dr. Anton Drager

A GATHERING OF EAGLES (Delbert Mann, USA, 1963), Colonel Jim
    Caldwell
MAN'S FAVORITE SPORT? (Howard Hawks, USA, 1964), Robert
    Willoughby
SEND ME NO FLOWERS (Norman Jewison, USA, 1964), George
    Kimball
STRANGE BEDFELLOWS (Melvin Frank, USA, 1965), Carter Harrison
A VERY SPECIAL FAVOR (Michael Gordon, USA, 1965), Paul
    Chadwick
BLINDFOLD (Philip Dunne, USA, 1965), Dr. Bartholomew Snow
SECONDS (John Frankenheimer, USA, 1966), Antioch Wilson
TOBRUK (Arthur Hiller, USA, 1967), Major Donald Craig
A FINE PAIR 'RUBA AL PROSSIMO TUO' (original title) (Francesco
    Maselli, Italy, 1968), Captain Mike Harmon
ICE STATION ZEBRA (John Sturges, USA, 1968), Commander James
    Ferraday
THE UNDEFEATED (Andrew V. McLaglen, USA, 1969), Col. James
    Langdon
DARLING LILI (Blake Edwards, USA, 1970), Major William Larrabee
HORNETS' NEST (Phil Karlson, Franco Cirino, USA, 1970), Turner
PRETTY MAIDS ALL IN A ROW (Roger Vadim, USA, 1971), Michael
    (Tiger) McDrew
SHOWDOWN (George Seaton, USA, 1973), Chuck Garvis
EMBRYO (Ralph Nelson, USA, 1976), Dr. Paul Holliston
AVALANCHE (Corey Allen, USA, 1978), David Shelby
THE MIRROR CRACK'D (Guy Hamilton, UK, 1980), Jason Rudd
THE DEVLIN CONNECTION III (Christian I. Nyby II, USA, 1982),
    Brian Devlin
THE AMBASSADOR (J. Lee Thompson, USA, 1984), Frank Stevenson
MOSCOW DOES NOT BELIEVE IN QUEERS (John Greyson, USA,
    1986), himself
ROCK HUDSON'S HOME MOVIES (Mark Rappaport, USA, 1992),
    himself

TV series

MCMILLAN & WIFE (Various, USA, 1971–7), Police Commissioner
    Stewart (Mac) McMillan
THE DEVLIN CONNECTION (Various, USA, 1982), Brian Devlin
DYNASTY (Various, USA, 1984–5), Daniel Reece

TV mini-series

WHEELS (Various, USA, 1978), Adam Trenton
THE MARTIAN CHRONICLES (Various, USA, 1980), Col. John Wilder

TV movies

THE STAR MAKER (Lou Antonio, USA, 1981), Danny Youngblood
WORLD WAR III (David Greene, Boris Sagal, USA, 1982), President
    Thomas McKenna
THE VEGAS STRIP WAR (George Englund, USA, 1984), Neil Chaine

INDEX

Notes: Page numbers in **bold** indicate detailed analysis. Those in *italic* refer to illustrations. *n* = endnote.

List of illustrations

While considerable effort has been made to correctly identify the copyright
holders, this has not been possible in all cases. We apologise for any apparent
negligence and any omissions or corrections brought to our attention will be
remedied in any future editions.

Bend of the River, © Universal Pictures Company; *Sea Devils*, © Coronado
Productions Ltd; *The Golden Blade*, Universal-International; *Magnificent
Obsession*, Universal Pictures Company/Universal-International; *Stage Fright*,
© Warner Bros. Pictures; *Written on the Wind*, © Universal Pictures Company;
Giant, © Giant Productions; *Ice Station Zebra*, © Metro-Goldwyn-Mayer;
Pillow Talk, © Arwin Productions; *A Very Special Favor*, Universal Pictures
Company/Lankershim Company; *Seconds*, © Paramount Pictures
Corporation/Joel Productions/Gibraltar Productions.